Varieties of Formal Languages

Varieties of Formal Languages

by

J. E. Pin

Translated by

A. Howie

English translation © 1986 North Oxford Academic Publishers Ltd

Original French language edition
(Variétés de langages formels) © 1984 Masson, Paris

Revised and updated 1986

English edition first published 1986
by North Oxford Academic Publishers Ltd,
a subsidiary of Kogan Page Ltd, 120 Pentonville Road,
London N1 9JN

Published in the United States of America by Plenum Press,
a Division of Plenum Publishing Corporation.
233 Spring Street
New York, NY 10013

Library of Congress Catalog Card Number

86-060593

ISBN 0-306-42294-8

Printed and bound in Great Britain.

Contents

vii

Preface

The theory of finite automata and of rational languages could be likened to the ground floor of a huge building under construction which is theoretical computer science. The metaphor would indicate first that it can be entered on the ground level and secondly that it is more convenient to go through it in order to reach the higher levels. It is also the first purely mathematical theory to emerge from the needs and intuitions of computer science in the wider sense. In fact, at the end of the 1950s Kleene, who was intrigued by electronic models of the nervous system which were then very fashionable, proposed characterizing feasible calculations by means of a system making use of a single bounded memory.

This led him to discover what are now called rational languages which are the subject of the present book by J. E. Pin. Subsequent work has revealed that this class is a particularly fundamental mathematical entity in the study of finite systems, for they appear quite naturally starting from considerations as diverse as those of restricted logical systems or the standard rational functions of analysis.

From the start, one of the principal problems was found to be a problem of classification, or rather of hierarchization. J. Rhodes showed that the composition of automata preserved the associated groups and McNaughton discovered that the existence of non-trivial groups of this kind was intimately related to the presence of loops within the system of calculation. The development by S. Eilenberg of the notion of *variety of language* gave a new impetus to research by coordinating these results with others such as the excellent theorem of Imre Simon. J. E. Pin has been one of the most active investigators in this area and we are indebted to him for numerous original contributions to the subject of varieties.

However, this rapid growth has necessitated a new synthesis incorporating the techniques discovered since the treatise of S. Eilenberg. J. E. Pin has undertaken this task and has been successful in presenting the subject with the care of an inspiring teacher, beginning with the most elementary aspects. Although it can easily be included in the more general framework of the theory of automata, it is an independent work, both of introduction and of preparation for research, which the author presents to the public interested in mathematics and in data processing.

M. P. SCHÜTZENBERGER
Professor in the University of Paris VII
Corresponding Member of the Academy of Sciences

Foreword

The aim of this book is to present the fundamental results of the theory of finite automata and of recognizable languages, or regular languages.

The concept of a finite automaton occurs frequently in computer science processing, whether it is used to model a particular machine, to formalize records of communication or to describe logic circuits. The notion of a recognizable language is equally fundamental: it enables us to take account of the linking of the calculations in a program, to express the behaviour of a process or to describe certain operations of a text editor and more generally to describe any iterative algorithm. Moreover, recognizable languages constitute the first link in a hierarchy of progressively more complex languages. Under this heading they were studied quite early: Kleene's theorem, on which the entire theory of finite automata is based, dates from 1956. Subsequently, the work of numerous investigators, in the first rank of whom appear M. P. Schützenberger, R. McNaughton, J. A. Brzozowski and I. Simon, has made clear the profound connections which exist between finite automata, recognizable languages and finite semigroups. The concept of variety of languages, which was introduced by Eilenberg in 1976, has enabled us to formalize this triple approach—automata, language and semigroups—and has provided a coherent and unified framework for the theory.

Since then the modern theory of automata has been constructed around this fundamental idea.

Thus the aim of this book is to present the theory of automata from the point of view of variety of languages. This approach has at least two advantages: it enables us to handle classical results in a concise and rigorous manner, and it facilitates access to the most recent results and problems. The first four chapters of the book are devoted to fundamental statements of the theory of automata. These theorems are proved at the same time (with the exception of Kleene's theorem, which is stated and admitted without proof) and illustrated by numerous examples. The final chapter presents a succinct review of the most recent results of the theory but contains no proofs.

The content of this book is approximately that of a course on DEA given at the University of Paris VI in the period 1981–1983. The level of presentation is thus that of an advanced graduate course. However, certain parts of the book—for example Chapter 1, part of Chapter 2 or the results in Chapter 4—can be used for a master's course on the theory of languages. The whole book should enable the reader to arrive quickly at the research level; thus the most important references are accompanied by a brief commentary aimed at facilitating the orientation of the reader. The reader of this book does not require any previous knowledge of formal languages or automata. However, it is necessary to have some familiarity with the formalism of algebra although, again, the previous theoretical knowledge required is limited to the notion of a group.

Chapter 0 defines the notation used in the book. Chapter 1 presents the basic material: semigroups, finite automata and recognizable languages. All the details of the algorithms for calculating the syntactic monoid of a language are also given in this chapter. Moreover, these algorithms have been implemented on a computer (APL programs of d'Autebert, Cousineau, Perrot and Rifflet). Chapter 2 is devoted to varieties. First the varieties of semigroups and of finite monoids are introduced, then their interpretation in terms of equations is given and finally Eilenberg's variety theorem is proved. Elementary examples of varieties of languages are presented at the end of the chapter. Chapter 3 is an introduction to the theory of finite semigroups. The subjects dealt with are Green's relations, simple and 0-simple semigroups, and the structure of regular $\mathscr{D}$-classes and of the minimal ideal of a finite semigroup. The algorithm for calculation of a regular $\mathscr{D}$-class is presented in detail and is illustrated by numerous examples. This algorithm has also been implemented on a computer (the APL programs of the authors cited above). We return to varieties of semigroups in the last two sections: the first presents the varieties of semigroups defined by Green's relations, and the second introduces relational morphisms and V-morphisms. The theorem of I. Simon on piecewise-testable languages and that of Schützenberger on star-free languages are proved in Chapter 4. Some applications of Simon's theorem to finite semigroups and the characterization of $\mathscr{R}$-trivial and $\mathscr{L}$-trivial languages are also included in this chapter. Chapter 5 presents various aspects of the theory of automata. The first section is devoted to operations on the languages: concatenation, mixing, star, morphisms, sequential functions etc. The second gives a résumé of recent work on hierarchies of languages—including the connection with symbolic logic—and the third presents the relations with the theory of variable-length codes. Finally the last section recalls briefly some other lines of research. The problems appearing at the end of the chapters are often the subjects of research. However, we have not given an indication of the difficulty of these problems except for problems which are open or have been recently solved—to determine the difficulty of a problem is itself a difficult problem.

I wish to thank in particular my friends S. W. Margolis, H. Straubing and D. Thérien for their numerous remarks and suggestions during the preparation of this book. I am also grateful to all the people who have read through or commented on various parts of the manuscript: J. Berstel, J. P. Pécuchet, D. Perrin, Ch. Reutenauer, G. Rindone, S. Schwer and W. Thomas as well as all the students on my course in Paris. I should like also to thank G. Lallement, J. F. Perrot and M. P. Schützenberger to whom I owe my interest in the theory of automata. Finally I thank Madame A. Dupont for her excellent work on the typing of the manuscript.

J. E. PIN

Introduction

Relations

This brief preliminary chapter is aimed at making precise certain definitions and properties referring to binary relations.

Let E and F be two sets. A **relation** between E and F is a subset R of $E \times F$. If $E = F$, we say that R is a relation on E. If $(u, v) \in E \times F$ we often write $u R v$ in place of $(u, v) \in R$. For example it is more convenient to write $2 \leq 3$ than $(2, 3) \in \leq$.

A relation R on a set E is **reflexive** if, for every $u \in E$, $u R u$. It is **symmetric** if, for every $(u, v) \in E \times E$, $u R v$ implies $v R u$. It is **transitive** if, for every $(u, v, w) \in E \times E \times E$, $u R v$ and $v R w$ imply $u R w$. It is **antisymmetric** if, for every $(u, v) \in E \times E$, $u R v$ and $v R u$ imply $u = v$. An **equivalence relation** is a relation which is simultaneously reflexive, symmetric and transitive. A **quasi-order relation** is a relation which is reflexive and transitive. A **partial order relation** is a relation which is reflexive, transitive and antisymmetric. A **total order relation** is an order relation such that, for every $(u, v) \in E \times E$, we have $u R v$ or $v R u$.

A (partial) function $\varphi : E \to F$ is a relation over $E \times F$ such that for every $x \in E$ there exists one and only one (in the case of a partial function, at most one) element $y \in F$ such that $(x, y) \in \varphi$. When this y exists, we denote it by $\varphi(x)$ or $x\varphi$. In this book we shall employ the notation $x\varphi$, which is more convenient in the theory of automata.

We can also consider each relation $R \subset E \times F$ in a dynamic way and associate with it the function τ from E into the set of subsets of F defined by

$$u\tau = \{v \in F | (u, v) \in R\}$$

Conversely, if τ is a function from E into the set of subsets of F, the **graph** R of τ, which is defined by

$$R = \{(u, v) \in E \times F | v \in u\tau\}$$

is a relation between E and F. By abuse of language, we say that $\tau : E \to F$ is a relation from E *into* F.

A relation $\tau : E \to F$ is called **injective** if, for every $u, v \in E$, $u\tau \cap v\tau \neq \varnothing$ implies $u = v$. In particular, if τ is a function, we find again the standard notion of an injective function. Moreover, τ is a **surjective** relation if, for every $v \in F$, there exists $u \in E$ such that $v \in u\tau$.

The relations over a set E are ordered by inclusion: if $R, S \subset E \times E$ are two relations, we say that R is **finer** than S (or that S is **coarser** than R) if $R \subset S$. In Chapter 4 we shall have to use the following elementary result.

Proposition 0.1

For every partial order relation R on a finite set E, there exists a total order relation on E which is coarser than R.

Proof

Put $S(R) = \{(a, b) \in E \times E | (a, b) \notin R$ and $(b, a) \notin R\}$. If $S(R) = \varnothing$, R is a total order. Otherwise fix $(a, b) \in S(R)$ and put $R' = R \cup \{(x, y) \in E \times E | (x, a) \in R$ and $(b, y) \in R\}$. Then R' is a partial ordering on E which is coarser than R. Since $(a, b) \in R'$, $S(R')$ is strictly included in $S(R)$ and we reach the conclusion by induction over the cardinality of $S(R)$.

Given a relation $\tau : E \to F$ which is a graph $R \subset E \times F$, we denote by $\tau^{-1} : F \to E$ the graph relation $R^{-1} = \{(v, u) \in F \times E | (u, v) \in R\}$. We can then see easily that, for every $v \in F$, $v\tau^{-1} = \{u \in E | v \in u\tau\}$.

More generally, if X is a subset of E, we put

$$X\tau = \bigcup_{x \in X} x\tau$$

If Y is a subset of F, we then have

$$Y\tau^{-1} = \bigcup_{y \in Y} y\tau^{-1} = \{u \in E | \text{there exists } y \in Y \text{ such that } y \in u\tau\}$$

i.e.

$$Y\tau^{-1} = \{u \in E | u\tau \cap Y \neq \varnothing\}$$

Given two relations $\tau_1 : E \to F$ and $\tau_2 : F \to G$, we denote by $\tau_1\tau_2$ the relation $E \to G$ defined, for every $u \in E$, by $u(\tau_1\tau_2) = \{w \in G | \text{there exists } v \in F \text{ such that } v \in u\tau_1 \text{ and } w \in v\tau_2\}$. In the case in which τ_1 and τ_2 are partial functions we find again the standard notion of the composition of two partial functions — up to the order of the factors — since we are using a 'post-fixed' notation. With a prefixed notation, we could write $\tau_2 \circ \tau_1$ in place of $\tau_1\tau_2$.

We now define some elementary properties which will frequently be used without reference in subsequent chapters. The proofs are immediate and are left to the reader.

Proposition 0.2

Let $\varphi : E \to F$ be a partial function. Then

(1) the relation φ^{-1} is injective;

(2) if φ is an injective function, φ^{-1} is an injective partial function and $\varphi\varphi^{-1}$ is the identity on E;

(3) if $\varphi : E \to F$ is a surjective partial function, then $\varphi^{-1}\varphi$ is the identity on F.

Proposition 0.3

Let $\tau: E \to F$ be a relation. Then for every $X, Y \subset E$, we have $(X \cup Y)\tau = X\tau \cup Y\tau$.

In the case in which τ is injective, we can be more precise.

Proposition 0.4

Let $\tau: E \to F$ be an injective relation (in particular $\tau = \varphi^{-1}$ where $\varphi: F \to E$ is a partial function). Then for every $X, Y \subset E$ we have

(1) $(X \cup Y)\tau = X\tau \cup Y\tau$
(2) $(X \cap Y)\tau = X\tau \cap Y\tau$
(3) $(X \setminus Y)\tau = X\tau \setminus Y\tau$

Proposition 0.5

Let $\varphi: E \to F$ be a surjective partial function. Then for every $X \subset E$ and $Y \subset F$, we have $X\varphi \cap Y = X\varphi \cap Y\varphi^{-1}\varphi = (X \cap Y\varphi^{-1})\varphi$.

Proposition 0.6

Let E, F, G be three sets and $\alpha: G \to E$, $\beta: G \to F$ be two functions. Suppose that α is surjective and that, for every $s, t \in G$, $s\alpha = t\alpha$ implies $s\beta = t\beta$. Then the relation $\alpha^{-1}\beta: E \to F$ is a function.

Apart from the 'post-fixed' notation used for functions and relations, we have followed the terminology and notation of M. Lothaire for everything that concerns free monoids and we have retained most of the notation of Eilenberg elsewhere. This notation is consistent with the notation regularly used in mathematics with one exception. The notation $\mathbb{Z}_p$ designates not the p-adic numbers but the group of integers modulo p which is regularly denoted by $\mathbb{Z}/p\mathbb{Z}$. Finally, following an abuse of notation which is quite widely accepted, we shall sometimes identify the singleton $\{s\}$ with the element s.

Chapter 1

Semigroups, Languages and Automata

The aim of this chapter is to give most of the definitions relating to the semigroups and languages which will be used in subsequent chapters. Some general statements on semigroups, almost all elementary, will also be found; the only difficult statement of this chapter is Theorem 1.10, which is a consequence of Ramsey's theorem. The second part of the chapter gives a brief résumé of the relations between automata, semigroups and languages. Finally, the last section is devoted to the explicit calculation of two syntactic semigroups.

1. Semigroups

1.1. Semigroups, monoids, morphisms

A **semigroup** is a couple formed from a set S and an internal associative law of composition defined on S. This law is generally denoted in a multiplicative way. Given two semigroups S and T, a semigroup morphism $\varphi: S \to T$ is a function from S into T such that, for all $x, y \in S, (xy)\varphi = (x\varphi)(y\varphi)$.

A **monoid** is a triplet formed from a set M, an internal associative law of composition defined over M and a distinct element of M, denoted by 1, such that, for every $x \in M$, $1x = x1 = x$. In practice, we usually denote the monoid (or semigroup) and the underlying set by the same letter. Given two monoids M and N, a monoid morphism $\varphi: M \to N$ is a function from M into N such that $1\varphi = 1$ and such that, for every $x, y \in M, (xy)\varphi = (x\varphi)(y\varphi)$. In the remainder of this book the word 'morphism' denotes, according to context, a semigroup morphism or a monoid morphism.

Given a semigroup S, we denote by S^1 the following monoid: if S is a monoid, $S^1 = S$; if S is not a monoid, $S^1 = S \cup \{1\}$ together with the law $*$ defined by $x * y = xy$ if $x, y \in S$ and $1 * x = x * 1 = x$ for every $x \in S^1$.

The semigroups (or monoids), together with the morphism which we have just defined, form a category. We shall see later that there exists another interesting category whose objects are semigroups and whose morphisms will be called 'relational morphisms'.

In agreement with the general definition, we say that a morphism $\varphi:S \to T$ is an isomorphism if there exists a morphism $\psi:T \to S$ such that $\varphi\psi = Id_S$ and $\psi\varphi = Id_T$. In fact a morphism is an isomorphism if and only if it is bijective. As a general rule we shall identify two isomorphic semigroups. This rule applies in particular to the definition of subsemigroups: we say that S is a **subsemigroup** of T if there exists an injective morphism $\varphi:S \to T$. S is then identified with $S\varphi$ together with the law induced by that of T. We shall say that T is a **quotient** of S if there exists a surjective morphism $\varphi:S \to T$.

A **submonoid** of a monoid M is a subsemigroup of M containing 1. If this submonoid is a group, we say that it is a **subgroup** of M. In particular the set U of invertible elements of M is the maximal subgroup of M, which is also called the group of **units** of M. The notion of a subgroup of a monoid must not be confused with that of a group within a **semigroup** S; a group *within* S is a subsemigroup of S which is a group.

We say that a semigroup S divides a semigroup T (notation $S < T$) if S is a quotient of a subsemigroup of T.

Proposition 1.1
The division relation is transitive.

Proof
Suppose $S_1 < S_2 < S_3$. Then there exists a subsemigroup T_1 of S_2, a subsemigroup T_2 of S_3 and surjective morphisms $\pi_1:T_1 \to S_1$ and $\pi_2:T_2 \to S_2$. Put $T = T_1\pi_2^{-1}$. Then T is a subsemigroup of S_3 and S_1 is a quotient of T since $T\pi_2\pi_1 = T_1\pi_1 = S_1$. Then S_1 divides S_3.

Given a family $(S_i)_{i \in I}$ of semigroups, the product

$$\prod_{i \in I} S_i$$

is the semigroup defined on the set

$$\prod_{i \in I} S_i$$

by the law $(s_i)_{i \in I} \cdot (s'_i)_{i \in I} = (s_i s'_i)_{i \in I}$. Since the semigroup 1 consisting of a single element is the identity with respect to the product operation, following the usual practice we put

$$\prod_{i \in \varnothing} S_i = 1$$

We note that the product of a family of monoids is a monoid.

A semigroup S is **generated** by a subset P of S if every element of S can be written in the form $p_1 \dots p_n$ with $n > 0$ and $p_1 \dots p_n \in P$.

1.2.   Idempotents, zero, ideal

An element e of a semigroup S is **idempotent** if $e = e^2$. We shall denote by $E(S)$ the set of idempotents of S. As we shall see, the idempotents play a fundamental role in the study of finite semigroups.

We call a **zero** of S an element, denoted by 0, such that $0s = s0 = 0$ for every $s \in S$. If S is a semigroup, we denote by S^0 the semigroup obtained from S by the addition of a zero: the support of S^0 is the disjoint union of S and the singleton $\{0\}$ and the law (here denoted $*$) is defined by $s * s' = ss'$ if $s, s' \in S$ and $s * 0 = 0 * s = 0$ for every $s \in S^0$.

A subset I of S is an **ideal**, a **right ideal** or a **left ideal** if $S^1 I S^1 \subset I$, $IS^1 \subset I$ or $S^1 I \subset I$ respectively.

A non-empty ideal I of a semigroup S is called **minimal** if, for every non-empty ideal J of S, $J \subset I$ implies $J = I$. We note that if such an ideal exists it is necessarily unique. The existence of a minimal ideal is assured in at least two important cases, namely if S is finite or if S possesses a zero. In this last case $\{0\}$ is the minimal ideal. A non-empty ideal $I \neq \{0\}$ such that, for every non-empty ideal J of S, $J \subset I$ implies $J = \{0\}$ or $J = I$ is called a **0-minimal ideal**. It should be noted that a semigroup can have several 0-minimal ideals.

1.3. Congruences

A **congruence** on a semigroup S is an equivalence relation $\sim$ on S compatible on the left and on the right with multiplication, i.e. such that, for every $a, b, c \in S$, $a \sim b$ implies $ac \sim bc$ and $ca \sim cb$. Classically the quotient set $S/\sim$ is then naturally provided with a semigroup structure. Three particular cases of congruences will be extensively used in the remainder of this book.

Rees congruence

Let I be an ideal of S and let $\equiv_I$ be the equivalence relation identifying all the elements of I and separating the other elements. Formally $s \equiv_I s'$ if and only if $s = s'$ or $s, s' \in I$. $\equiv_I$ is then a congruence called the Rees congruence. Traditionally we write S/I for the quotient of S by $\equiv_I$.

Syntactic congruence

Let P be a subset of S and $\equiv$ be an equivalence relation over S. We say that $\equiv$ saturates P if P is the union of classes modulo $\equiv$, which amounts to saying that, for every $u, v \in S$, $u \equiv v$ and $u \in P$ imply $v \in P$. The **syntactic congruence** of P is the congruence $\sim_P$ over S defined by $u \sim_P v$ if and only if, for every $s, t \in S^1$, ($sut \in P \Leftrightarrow svt \in P$). We can show (this is left as an exercise) that $\sim_P$ is the coarsest congruence saturating P. This congruence is particularly important in the theory of languages as we shall see a little later.

Nuclear congruence

Let $\varphi : S \to T$ be a semigroup morphism. We denote by $\sim_\varphi$ the (nuclear) congruence associated with φ and defined by

$$u \sim_\varphi v \text{ if and only if } u\varphi = v\varphi$$

We then have the classical result.

Proposition 1.2

Let $\varphi: S \to T$ be a semigroup morphism and $\pi: S \to S/\sim_\varphi$ be the natural projection. Then there exists a unique morphism $\bar{\varphi}: S/\sim_\varphi \to T$ such that $\varphi = \pi\bar{\varphi}$. Moreover, $\bar{\varphi}$ is an isomorphism of $S/\sim_\varphi$ over $S\varphi$.

Proof

The situation is summed up in the following diagram:

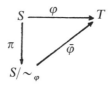

Necessarily $\bar{\varphi} = \pi^{-1}\varphi$. It is now necessary to verify that $\bar{\varphi}$ is indeed a morphism. Now if $u, v \in s\pi^{-1}\varphi$, there exists $x, y \in s\pi^{-1}$ such that $x\varphi = u$ and $y\varphi = v$. Since $x, y \in s\pi^{-1}$, $x \sim_\varphi y$, i.e. $x\varphi = y\varphi$. Thus $\bar{\varphi}$ is a function. Moreover, if $x_1 \in s_1\pi^{-1}$ and $x_2 \in s_2\pi^{-1}$, it follows that $x_1 x_2 \in (s_1 s_2)\pi^{-1}$ whence

$$(s_1\bar{\varphi})(s_2\bar{\varphi}) = (x_1\varphi)(x_2\varphi) = (x_1 x_2)\varphi = (s_1 s_2)\bar{\varphi}$$

$\bar{\varphi}$ is injective; if $s_1\bar{\varphi} = s_2\bar{\varphi}$, there exists $x_1 \in s_1\pi^{-1}$ and $x_2 \in s_2\pi^{-1}$ such that $x_1\varphi = x_2\varphi$. Hence we can deduce $x_1 \sim_\varphi x_2$, i.e. $x_1\pi = x_2\pi$, whence $s_1 = s_2$. Then $\bar{\varphi}$ induces an isomorphism of $S/\sim_\varphi$ over its image $(S/\sim_\varphi)\bar{\varphi} = S\varphi$.

Let $(\sim_i)_{i \in I}$ be a family of congruences over a semigroup S. We denote by $\sim$ the intersection of the family $(\sim_i)_{i \in I}$; by definition $u \sim v$ if and only if, for every $i \in I$, $u \sim_i v$.

Proposition 1.3

With the preceding notation $S/\sim$ is a subsemigroup of

$$\prod_{i \in I} S/\sim_i$$

Proof

We denote by $\pi_i: S \to S/\sim_i$ the projections and by

$$\pi: S \to \prod_{i \in I} S/\sim_i$$

the morphism defined by $s\pi = (s\pi_i)_{i \in I}$ for every $s \in S$. The nuclear congruence of π is none other than $\sim$, and thus $S/\sim$ is isomorphic to $S\pi$ in accordance with Proposition 1.2.

Proposition 1.4

Let $\sim_1$ and $\sim_2$ be two congruences defined over a semigroup S. We suppose that, for every $s, t \in S$, $s \sim_1 t$ implies $s \sim_2 t$. Then $S/\sim_2$ is a quotient of $S/\sim_1$.

Proof

We denote by $\pi_1:S \to S/\sim_1$ and $\pi_2:S \to S/\sim_2$ the canonical morphisms. The condition of the statement implies that $\pi = \pi_1^{-1}\pi_2$ is a surjective morphism $S/\sim_1 \to S/\sim_2$.

1.4. Semigroups of transformations

If E is a set, we denote by $\mathcal{T}(E)$ the monoid of functions from E into E together with the composition of functions. If $E = \{1,\dots,n\}$, we generally write $\mathcal{T}_n$ for the monoid $\mathcal{T}(E)$.

A transformation semigroup over E is a subsemigroup of $\mathcal{T}(E)$. The importance of transformation semigroups is emphasized by the following proposition.

Proposition 1.5

Every semigroup is isomorphic to a transformation semigroup. In particular every finite semigroup S is isomorphic to a subsemigroup of $\mathcal{T}_n$ for a certain integer n.

Proof

We associate with each element s of S the right translation $\rho_s:S^1 \to S^1$ defined by $a\rho_s = as$ for every $a \in S^1$. We can easily verify that the function $s \to \rho_s$ thus defined is an injective morphism from S into $\mathcal{T}(S^1)$.

There follows another elementary theorem; it is concerned with the structure of semigroups generated by a single element (sometimes called **monogenic** semigroups).

Proposition 1.6

Let S be a semigroup generated by an element a. Then either $S = (\mathbb{N}\setminus\{0\}, +)$ or S is finite. In the latter case there exist integers $n \geq 0$ and $p > 0$ such that $a^n = a^{n+p}$ and $S = \{a, a^2, \dots, a^{n+p-1}\}$. Then S contains a single idempotent, which is the identity of the group $G = \{a^n, a^{n+1}, \dots, a^{n+p-1}\}$.

Proof

If all the powers of a are distinct we clearly find ourselves in the first case. Otherwise let n be the smallest positive integer such that there exists k satisfying $a^n = a^{n+k}$ and let us write p for the smallest k satisfying this last relation. Then all the elements $a, a^2, \ldots a^{n+p-1}$ are distinct. Moreover, if $m \geq p$, we have $m = qp + r$ with $q \geq 1$ and $0 \leq r < p$ whence $a^{n+m} = a^{n+qp+r} = a^{n+r}$. We can deduce from this that $S = \{a, a^2, \ldots, a^{n+p-1}\}$. Finally, let $G = \{a^n, \ldots, a^{n+p-1}\}$ and $\varphi: G \to \mathbb{Z}_p$ defined by $(a^{n+i})\varphi = n + i \pmod p$. The function φ is an isomorphism of G over $\mathbb{Z}_p$ and consequently G contains a (unique) idempotent. Since every element of S has a power in G, S itself contains exactly one idempotent.

Corollary 1.7
Every non-empty finite semigroup contains an idempotent.

1.5. Free semigroups
Let A be a set called an alphabet, whose elements are called letters. We shall denote by A^+ and A^* respectively the free semigroup or monoid over A. In practice A^+ is constructed in the following way. The elements of A^+ are the non-empty finite sequences of letters called words. For simplicity, we shall denote them by simple juxtaposition: $a_1 \ldots a_n$. Now the product of two words $a_1 \ldots a_p$ and $b_1 \ldots b_q$ is the word $a_1 \ldots a_p b_1 \ldots b_q$. In the case of a free monoid we must add the empty word (denoted by 1) which corresponds to the empty sequence. The universal property of the free semigroup (or monoid) over A can then be expressed as follows.

Proposition 1.8
If $\varphi: A \to S$ is a function from A into a semigroup (or monoid) S there exist unique morphisms $\bar{\varphi}: A^+ \to S$ (or $\varphi: A^* \to S$) such that $a\varphi = a\bar{\varphi}$ for every $a \in A$. Moreover $\bar{\varphi}$ is surjective if and only if $A\varphi$ is a generator set of S.

We can deduce in particular from this that every semigroup (or monoid) is the quotient of a free semigroup (or monoid). We can also deduce from this that there exists one and only one morphism, denoted by $| \ |$, of A^* in $\mathbb{N}$ satisfying $|a| = 1$ for every $a \in A$. We can see that, if $w = a_1 \ldots a_n$, we have $|w| = n$; $|w|$ is by definition the length of w. There follows another consequence of this proposition.

Proposition 1.9
Let $\eta: A^+ \to S$ be a morphism and $\beta: T \to S$ a surjective morphism. Then there exists a morphism $\varphi: A^+ \to T$ such that $\eta = \varphi\beta$.

Proof
Let us associate with each letter $a \in A$ an element $a\varphi$ of $a\eta\beta^{-1}$. We thus define a function $\varphi: A \to T$ which can be extended to a morphism $\varphi: A^+ \to T$ such that $\eta = \varphi\beta$.

The proposition which follows rests on a celebrated combinatorial theorem, due to Ramsey, which we shall admit without proof. We call a colouring of a set E in m colours a function from E into $\{1, \ldots, m\}$.

Theorem 1.10 (Ramsey)

Let r, k, m be integers satisfying $k \geq r, m > 0$. Then there exists an integer $N = R(r, k, m)$ such that for every finite set E having at least N elements and for every colouring in m colours of the subsets of E having r elements there exists a subset of E with k elements of which all the subsets with r elements have the same colour.

Let S be a non-empty finite semigroup and let A be a set in one-to-one correspondence with S. We shall denote by $u \to \bar{u}$ the surjective morphism $A^+ \to S$ induced by this correspondence.

Theorem 1.11

Let S be a non-empty finite semigroup and let $k \geq 2$ be an integer. Then there exists an integer $n = n(S, k)$ such that, for every word w of A^+ of length greater than or equal to n, there exists an idempotent $e \in S$ and a factorization $w = x u_1 \ldots u_k y$ with $x, y \in A^*, u_1, \ldots, u_k \in A^+$ and $\bar{u}_1 = \ldots = \bar{u}_k = e$.

Proof

Put $n = R(2, k + 1, \text{card}(S))$ and let $w = a_1 \ldots a_n w'$ be a word of length greater than or equal to n (the a_i are naturally letters of the alphabet A). We define a colouring into $\text{card}(S)$ colours of pairs of elements of $\{1, \ldots, n\}$ in the following way: the colour of $\{i, j\}$ (where $i < j$) is the element $\bar{a}_i \ldots \bar{a}_{j-1}$ of S. According to Ramsey's theorem, we can find $k + 1$ indices $i_0 < i_1 \ldots < i_k$ such that all the pairs of elements of $\{i_0, \ldots, i_k\}$ have the same colour. In particular since $k \geq 2$

$$\bar{a}_{i_0} \ldots \bar{a}_{i_1 - 1} = \bar{a}_{i_1} \ldots \bar{a}_{i_2 - 1} = \ldots = \bar{a}_{i_{k-1}} \ldots \bar{a}_{i_k - 1} = e = \overline{\bar{a}_{i_0} \ldots \bar{a}_{i_2 - 1}}$$

We can deduce from this that $e = e^2$ and we obtain the required factorization by taking $x = a_1 \ldots a_{i_0 - 1}, u_j = a_{i_{j-1}} \ldots a_{i_j - 1}$ for $1 \leq j \leq k$ and $y = a_{i_k} \ldots a_n w'$.

We can in fact prove Theorem 1.11 directly without using Theorem 1.10. However, we have preferred to use Ramsey's theorems for two reasons. Firstly, the proof of Theorem 1.11 becomes short and elegant. Secondly, Ramsey's theorem is a result which it is important to know and which has other applications in the theory of semigroups (see Problem 1.5 for example). It is also the starting point of numerous investigations in combinatorics (see the book *Ramsey Theory* by Graham, Rothschild and Spencer).

The following statement is similar to the preceding one but is simpler to prove. If S is a semigroup and n is a positive integer, we write

$$S^n = \{s_1 \ldots s_n \mid s_i \in S \text{ for } 1 \leq i \leq n\}$$

Proposition 1.12

Let S be a finite semigroup and let $E(S)$ be the set of idempotents of S. Then $S^n = SE(S)S$ for every $n \geq \text{card}(S)$.

Proof

The result is obvious if $S = \varnothing$. Suppose that S is non-empty and let $s \in S^n$ with

$n \geq \operatorname{card}(S)$; then there exists a word w of length n such that $\bar{w} = s$. For $1 \leq i \leq n$, w admits a factorization $w = u_i v_i$ with $|u_i| = i$. If the elements $\bar{u}_i$ are all distinct, then $n = \operatorname{card}(S)$ and one of the $\bar{u}_i$ is an idempotent e of S. Then $\bar{u}_i e = \bar{u}_i$ in this case. If there exist two indices $i < j$ such that $\bar{u}_i = \bar{u}_j$, then by putting $u_j = u_i z$ it follows that $\bar{u}_i \bar{z} = \bar{u}_i$ and therefore $\bar{u}_i \bar{z}^k = \bar{u}_i$ for every k. According to Proposition 1.6 there exists an integer m such that $\bar{z}^m = e$ is idempotent. We then have $\bar{u}_i e = \bar{u}_i$ in this case also. Finally it follows that $s = \bar{u}_i \bar{v}_i = \bar{u}_i e \bar{v}_i \in SE(S)S$.

2. Languages

2.1. Words

Let A be an alphabet. A **word** is an element of the free monoid A^*. If w is a word and a is a letter, we write $|w|_a$ for the number of occurrences of the letter a in the word w. We then have

$$\sum_{a \in A} |w|_a = |w|$$

where $|w|$ is the length of w.

A word w is called **multilinear** if for every letter $a \in A$ we have $|w|_a \leq 1$. It is called **primitive** if w is not the power of another word, i.e. if $w = u^n$ implies $n = 1$. A word u is a **left factor** (or **prefix**) of w if there exists a word v such that $uv = w$. If $v \neq 1$, we say that u is a **left proper factor** of w. We define the notion of a **right factor** (or **suffix**) in a similar way. A word u is a **factor** of a word v if there exist words x and y such that $v = xuy$. u is a **proper factor** if $xy \neq 1$. A word $u = a_1 \ldots a_n$ (where $a_1, \ldots, a_n$ are letters) is a **subword** of v if there exist words $v_0, \ldots, v_n \in A^*$ such that $v = v_0 a_1 v_1 a_2 \ldots a_n v_n$. The first letter of a non-empty word is called the **initial**, and the last letter is called the **ending**.

Example

Let $u = abacbacb$. Then aba is a left factor of u, acb is a right factor, $bacb$ is a factor and $bcbb$ is a subword of u.

We refer the reader who is interested in combinatorics on words to the book *Combinatorics on Words* by M. Lothaire. He will find there in particular a proof of the following property, which is given here by way of an exercise. Let u and v be two non-empty words. Then the following conditions are equivalent:

(1) u and v commute, i.e. $uv = vu$;
(2) there exist $n, m > 0$ such that $u^n = v^m$;
(3) u and v are powers of one and the same word.

2.2. Automata

We call a triplet $\mathscr{A} = (Q, A, \cdot)$, where Q is a set (or a finite set) called a set of states, A is a finite alphabet and $\cdot$ denotes an action $Q \times A \to Q$, an automaton (or a finite automaton). By associativity we extend the action to A^* starting from the following rules, where $q \in Q$, $w \in A^*$ and $a \in A$:

$$q \cdot 1 = q$$
$$q \cdot (wa) = (q \cdot w) \cdot a$$

Example 2.1

For $Q = \{1, 2, 3\}$, $A = \{a, b\}$

$$1 \cdot a = 2 \quad 2 \cdot a = 3 \quad 3 \cdot a = 3$$
$$1 \cdot b = 1 \quad 2 \cdot b = 1 \quad 3 \cdot b = 3$$

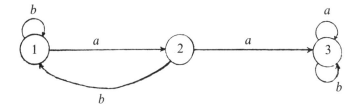

$$2 \cdot babaab = 3$$

Each word w of A^* thus defines a function from Q into Q. The monoid generated by all the functions thus defined (w varying over A^*) is a submonoid of $\mathcal{T}(Q)$; it is the **transition monoid** $M(\mathscr{A})$ of the automaton $\mathscr{A}$. Clearly $M(\mathscr{A})$ is generated by the functions defined by the letters of the alphabet and we have a canonical morphism $A^* \to M(\mathscr{A})$.

Example 2.1 (continued)

generators		1	2	3
	a	2	3	3
	b	1	1	3
	a^2	3	3	3
	ab	1	3	3
	ba	2	2	3

The continuation of the calculation shows that b, b^2 and bab define the same function from Q into Q, in the same way as $a^2, a^3, a^2 b, ba^2$ on the one hand and a, aba on the other. The transition monoid $M(\mathscr{A})$ thus contains six elements corresponding to the words $1, a, b, a^2, ab$ and ba.

2.3.   Rational and recognizable languages

Let A be a finite alphabet. We call a **language** (over the alphabet A) a subset of the free monoid A^*. We can define a large number of operations over languages. Apart from the classical boolean operations (finite union, finite intersection, complementation) we shall use principally the product, the star and the quotient. The (concatenation) **product** of two languages L and K of A^* is the language

$$LK = \{uv \in A^* | u \in L \quad \text{and} \quad v \in K\}$$

The **star** of a language L of A^*, denoted by L^*, is by definition the submonoid of A^* generated by L. Finally if K and L are two languages of A^* we call the left (or right) **quotient** or **residual** of L by K the language $K^{-1}L$ (or LK^{-1}) which is defined by

$$K^{-1}L = \{v \in A^* | Kv \cap L \neq \varnothing\} = \{v \in A^* | \text{there exists } u \in K \text{ such that } uv \in L\}$$

and similarly

$$LK^{-1} = \{v \in A^* | vK \cap L \neq \varnothing\} = \{v \in A^* | \text{there exists } u \in K \text{ such that } vu \in L\}$$

By abuse of notation, we often identify the word $u \in A^*$ and the language $\{u\}$. The operations stated above enable us to express simply certain languages defined by combinatorial properties. For example, if $A = \{a, b\}$, the set of words commencing with the letter a and having no factor equal to aba is the language $L = aA^* \setminus A^*abaA^*$. A moment's reflection will convince the reader that the same language can be expressed in the form $L = a(a \cup bbb^*a)^*b^*$. We can now indicate in a precise way the power of the operations which we have introduced. We start with some definitions.

Definition 2.1
Let A be a finite alphabet. The set of **rational languages** of A^* is the smallest set, denoted by $A^*\mathscr{R}\text{at}$, of languages of A^* such that

(a) for every word $u \in A^*$, $\{u\} \in A^*\mathscr{R}\text{at}$,
(b) $A^*\mathscr{R}\text{at}$ is closed under finite union, product and star.

We note that the empty set is a rational language since

$$\varnothing = \bigcup_{i \in \varnothing} L_i$$

Definition 2.2
Let A be a finite alphabet, $\eta : A^* \to M$ a monoid morphism and $L \subset A^*$ a language. We say that η **recognizes** L if there exists a subset P of M such that $L = P\eta^{-1}$. By extension, we say also in this case that M recognizes L.

Definition 2.3
A language is called **recognizable** if it is recognized by a finite monoid.

The last two definitions are connected with the notion of an automaton in the following way. Let A be a finite alphabet and $\mathscr{A} = (Q, A, \cdot)$ an automaton. We say that the language L is **recognized by the automaton** $\mathscr{A}$ if there exists a state $q_0 \in Q$ (called the **initial** state) and a set of states F (the set of **final** states) such that $u \in L$ if and only if $q_0 \cdot u \in F$.

Example 2.2

Taking $q_0 = 1$ and $F = \{3\}$, we can see that the automaton of Example 2.1 recognizes the language $L = A^*aaA^*$.

The connection between a monoid and an automaton is made clear by the following proposition.

Proposition 2.1

If $L \subset A^*$ is recognized by an automaton, it is recognized by the transition monoid of this automaton. Moreover, L is recognized by a finite automaton if and only if L is recognizable.

Proof

Let $\mathscr{A}$ be an automaton recognizing L and possessing the initial state q_0 and the set of final states F. We denote by $\eta: A^* \to M(\mathscr{A})$ the canonical morphism, and we put $P = L\eta$. We shall show that $P\eta^{-1} = L$. Let $u \in P\eta^{-1}$; then $u\eta \in P = L\eta$ by definition and therefore $u\eta = v\eta$ for a certain $v \in L$. This means that u and v define the same function from the set of states into itself. In particular $q_0 \cdot u = q_0 \cdot v$ and, since $v \in L$, $q_0 \cdot v \in F$. Therefore $q_0 \cdot u \in F$ and we can deduce from this that $u \in L$. Thus we have just established the inclusion $L\eta\eta^{-1} \subset L$. The opposite inclusion is obvious and therefore $L = P\eta^{-1}$ as stated. Thus $M(\mathscr{A})$ recognizes L.

In particular if $\mathscr{A}$ is a finite automaton, L is recognized by the finite monoid $M(\mathscr{A})$ and L is recognizable. Conversely, if L is recognizable there exist a finite monoid M, a morphism $\eta: A^* \to M$ and a subset of M such that $P\eta^{-1} = L$. Let $\mathscr{A}_M = (M, A, \cdot)$ be the automaton defined by the operation $m \cdot a = m(a\eta)$. If we take 1 as the initial state and P as the set of final states, the automaton $\mathscr{A}_M$ recognizes L since

$$1 \cdot u \in P \Leftrightarrow 1(u\eta) \in P \Leftrightarrow u \in P\eta^{-1}$$

Thus L is recognized by a finite automaton.

The statements which follow express in terms of monoids some quite classical results of the theory of automata.

Proposition 2.2

Let L be a language of A^*. If M recognizes L, M recognizes $A^* \setminus L$.

Proof

Let $\eta: A^* \to M$ and $P \subset M$ be such that $L = P\eta^{-1}$. Then $(M \setminus P)\eta^{-1} = A^* \setminus L$.

Proposition 2.3

Let L_1 and L_2 be two languages of A^* recognized respectively by the monoids M_1 and M_2. Then $L_1 \cap L_2$ and $L_1 \cup L_2$ are recognized by $M_1 \times M_2$.

Proof

Let $\eta_1:A^* \to M_1$, $\eta_2:A^* \to M_2$, $P_1 \subset M_1$ and $P_2 \subset M_2$ be such that $L_1 = P_1\eta_1^{-1}$ and $L_2 = P_2\eta_2^{-1}$. Let $\eta:A^* \to M_1 \times M_2$ be the morphism defined by $u\eta = (u\eta_1, u\eta_2)$. We then have the formulae

$$(P_1 \times P_2)\eta^{-1} = L_1 \cap L_2$$

and

$$((P_1 \times M_2) \cup (M_1 \times P_2))\eta^{-1} = L_1 \cup L_2$$

Proposition 2.4

Let $\varphi:A^* \to B^*$ be a morphism of free monoids and $L \subset B^*$ a language recognized by a monoid M. Then M recognizes $L\varphi^{-1}$ also.

Proof

Let $\eta:B^* \to M$ and $P \subset M$ be such that $L = P\eta^{-1}$. Then $L\varphi^{-1} = (P\eta^{-1})\varphi^{-1} = P(\varphi\eta)^{-1}$, which proves that $L\varphi^{-1}$ is recognized by the morphism $\varphi\eta:A^* \to M$.

Proposition 2.5

Let K and L be two languages of A^*. If M recognizes L, M recognizes $K^{-1}L$ and LK^{-1}.

Proof

Let $\eta:A^* \to M$ and $P \subset M$ be such that $P\eta^{-1} = L$. Put

$$Q = \{m \in M \mid \exists u \in K \, (u\eta)m \in P\}$$

It follows that

$$\begin{aligned} Q\eta^{-1} &= \{v \in A^* \mid v\eta \in Q\} \\ &= \{v \in A^* \mid \exists u \in K \, (u\eta)(v\eta) \in P\} \\ &= \{v \in A^* \mid \exists u \in K \, (uv)\eta \in P\} \\ &= \{v \in A^* \mid \exists u \in K \, uv \in L\} \\ &= K^{-1}L \end{aligned}$$

Then $K^{-1}L$ is recognized by M. The proof for LK^{-1} is similar.

We denote by $A^*\mathscr{R}\text{ec}$ the set of recognizable languages of A^*. We can then state the following proposition.

Proposition 2.6

(1) For every alphabet A, $A^*\mathscr{R}\text{ec}$ is a boolean algebra.
(2) If $L \in A^*\mathscr{R}\text{ec}$ and $K \subset A^*$ then $K^{-1}L, LK^{-1} \in A^*\mathscr{R}\text{ec}$.
(3) If $\varphi:A^* \to B^*$ is a morphism of free monoids and if $L \in B^*\mathscr{R}\text{ec}$, then $L\varphi^{-1} \in A^*\mathscr{R}\text{ec}$.

Proof

This follows from Propositions 2.2–2.5.

We can now state a fundamental result of the theory of languages, i.e. the theorem of Kleene. We shall accept this theorem — the proof appears in most of the books devoted to the theory of automata or languages (e.g. Eilenberg, Vol. 1, Chapter 7, or Lallement, Chapter 6).

Theorem (Kleene)

Let A be a finite alphabet. A language $L \subset A^*$ is rational if and only if it is recognizable.

It follows in particular from Kleene's theorem that the set of rational languages of A^* is closed under finite boolean operations and under left (or right) quotient by an arbitrary language.

2.4. Syntactic monoids

Let L be a language of A^*. In agreement with the general definition, we call a syntactic congruence of L a congruence $\sim_L$ defined over A^* by $u \sim_L v$ if and only if, for every $x, y \in A^*$, $xuy \in L \Leftrightarrow xvy \in L$. The **syntactic monoid** of L is the quotient monoid $M(L) = A^*/\sim_L$. The proposition which follows shows that the syntactic monoid of a language L is the smallest monoid recognizing L, where 'smallest' is taken in the sense of the division relation.

Proposition 2.7

Let L be a language of A^*.

(1) M recognizes L if and only if $M(L)$ divides M.
(2) If M recognizes L and if M divides N, N recognizes L.

Proof

(a) First, $M(L)$ recognizes L. Indeed we denote by $\eta: A^* \to A^*/\sim_L = M(L)$ the canonical morphism. We shall show that $L = L\eta\eta^{-1}$. The inclusion from left to right is obvious. Conversely let $u \in L\eta\eta^{-1}$. Then $u\eta \in L\eta$ and there exists $v \in L$ such that $u\eta = v\eta$, i.e. $u \sim_L v$. Since $v \in L$ we also have $u \in L$, by taking $x = y = 1$ in the definition of $\sim_L$. Putting $P = L\eta$, we find $P\eta^{-1} = L$ and therefore $M(L)$ recognizes L.

(b) Suppose that $M(L)$ divides M. Then there exist a monoid N, an injective morphism $\alpha: N \to M$ and a surjective morphism $\beta: N \to M(L)$. According to Proposition 1.9, there exists a morphism $\varphi: A^* \to N$ such that $\eta = \varphi\beta$. Put $P = L\eta\beta^{-1}\alpha \subset M$. It follows that

$$
\begin{array}{c}
A^* \\
\eta \downarrow \quad \overset{\varphi}{\searrow} \\
\quad \quad N \overset{\alpha}{\longrightarrow} M \\
\quad \quad \nearrow \beta \\
M(L)
\end{array}
$$

$$P(\varphi\alpha)^{-1} = P\alpha^{-1}\varphi^{-1} = L\eta\beta^{-1}\alpha\alpha^{-1}\varphi^{-1} = L\eta\beta^{-1}\varphi^{-1} = L\eta\eta^{-1} = L$$

Thus M recognizes L.

(c) Finally suppose that M recognizes L. Then there exist a morphism $\varphi:A^* \to M$ and a subset P of M such that $L = P\varphi^{-1}$. Put $N = A^*\varphi$; N is a submonoid of M. Suppose that $u\varphi = v\varphi$ and $xuy \in L$. Then $(xuy)\varphi = (xvy)\varphi \in L\varphi = P$ and therefore $xvy \in L$ since $P\varphi^{-1} = L$. It follows from this that $u\varphi = v\varphi$ implies $u \sim_L v$. According to Proposition 1.4, there exists a surjective morphism $\pi:N \to A^*/\sim_L = M(L)$. Therefore $M(L)$ divides M. This proves (1). Part (2) of the statement results from part (1).

Corollary 2.8
Let L, L_1 and L_2 be recognizable languages of A^* and let K be an arbitrary language. Then

(a) $M(A^* \setminus L) = M(L)$
(b) $M(L_1 \cap L_2)$ divides $M(L_1) \times M(L_2)$
(c) $M(L_1 \cup L_2)$ divides $M(L_1) \times M(L_2)$
(d) $M(LK^{-1})$ and $M(K^{-1}L)$ divide $M(L)$
(e) if $\varphi:B^* \to A^*$ is a morphism of free monoids, $M(L\varphi^{-1})$ divides $M(L)$

Proof
This is an immediate consequence of Propositions 2.2–2.6.

The link between syntactic monoids and automata is the following. We call the minimal automaton of a language L the automaton $\mathscr{A} = (Q, A, \cdot)$ defined thus: the set of states is $Q = \{u^{-1}L \mid u \in A^*\}$ and the transitions are given by

$$(u^{-1}L) \cdot a = a^{-1}(u^{-1}L) = (ua)^{-1}L \quad \text{for all } a \in A$$

We can then show that the transition monoid of the minimal automaton of L is equal to the syntactic monoid of L.

It is easy to see that the minimal automaton of L recognizes L by taking as the initial state $q_0 = L$ and as the set of final states $F = \{u^{-1}L \mid u \in L\}$. Moreover, the term 'minimal' corresponds to a property in the theory of automata. On the one hand the minimal automaton is **accessible** which means that, for every state q, there exists a word $u \in A^*$ such that $q_0 \cdot u = q$. On the other hand this is the smallest accessible automaton recognizing L. More precisely, if $\mathscr{A}' = (Q', A, \cdot)$ possessing an initial state q'_0 and a set of final states F' is an accessible automaton recognizing L, there exists a unique surjective function $\varphi:Q' \to Q$ such that $q_0\varphi = q'_0$ and such that, for every word $u \in A^*$, $(q \cdot u)\varphi = (q\varphi) \cdot u$.

2.5. Codes
Codes are particular languages which we shall use in this book mainly by way of examples or exercises. The reader interested in the theory of codes should refer to the book by Berstel, Perrin and Schützenberger on this subject.

We say that a language X of A^* is a **code** if the submonoid of A^* generated by X is free from the base X. Equivalently, X is a code if, for every $n, m \geq 1$ and for every $x_1, \ldots, x_n, x_1', \ldots, x_m' \in X$, the condition $x_1 \ldots x_n = x_1' \ldots x_m'$ implies $n = m$

and $x_i = x_i'$ for $1 \leq i \leq n$. X is respectively a **prefix code** or a **suffix code** if X does not contain the empty word and if no word of X is respectively a left proper factor or a right proper factor of another word of X, i.e. if, for every $u, v \in A^*$, $u \in X$ and $uv \in X$ (or $vu \in X$) implies $v = 1$. It can be shown that a submonoid P of A^* is generated by a prefix code or a suffix code respectively if and only if, for every $u, v \in A^*$, the conditions $u \in P$ and $uv \in P$ (or $vu \in P$) imply $v \in P$. It is easy to see that every prefix code or suffix code is a code. A code which is simultaneously prefix and suffix is called **biprefix**.

Example 2.3
If $A = \{a, b\}$, the languages $X = \{a, ba, b^2\}$ and $Y = \{a^2, ab^2, ba\}$ are prefix codes. The language Y is even a biprefix code. However, X is not a suffix code because a is a suffix of ba.

It is convenient to represent finite prefix codes by a diagram. For this, we represent the letters of the alphabet by segments of various slopes and words by concatenation of these segments.

Example 2.4
Let $A = \{a, b\}$. We associate with the letter a the segment $/$ and with the letter b the segment $\backslash$. The word $abba$ is then represented by

and the word $bbab$ is represented by

Prefix codes are then represented by 'trees'.

Example 2.5
If $A = \{a, b\}$, $\{a, ba, b^2\}$ is represented by

and $\{a^2, aba, b^2\}$ is represented by

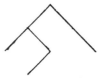

If $A = \{a, b, c\}$, $\{aba, ab^2, abc, ca, cb\}$ is represented by

2.6.   The case of free semigroups

All that we have discussed can be adapted without difficulty to the case in which the languages are subsets of the free semigroup A^+. We define in a similar way the notions of minimal automaton, syntactic semigroup, transition semigroup and recognizable language. The rule is to replace everywhere the term monoid by semigroup and $*$ by $+$. There is an exception to this rule: the definition of the syntactic congruence of a language L of A^+. In fact since $A^* = (A^+)^1$, this definition is as follows: $u \sim_L v$ if and only if, for every $x, y \in A^*$, $(xuy \in L \Leftrightarrow xvy \in L)$.

3.   Explicit calculations

During the calculation of residuals, we can use the following formulae, whose demonstration is left to the reader. In these formulae a designates a letter, u and v designate words and L, L_1, L_2 designate languages.

$$u^{-1}(L_1 \cup L_2) = u^{-1}L_1 \cup u^{-1}L_2$$
$$u^{-1}(L_1 \setminus L_2) = u^{-1}L_1 \setminus u^{-1}L_2$$
$$u^{-1}(L_1 \cap L_2) = u^{-1}L_1 \cap u^{-1}L_2$$
$$a^{-1}(L_1 L_2) \begin{cases} = (a^{-1}L_1)L_2 & \text{if } 1 \notin L_1 \\ = (a^{-1}L_1)L_2 \cup a^{-1}L_2 & \text{if } 1 \in L_1 \end{cases}$$
$$a^{-1}L^* = (a^{-1}L)L^*$$
$$v^{-1}(u^{-1}L) = (uv)^{-1}L$$

3.1. Syntactic semigroup of $L = A^*abaA^*$ over the alphabet $A = \{a, b\}$

We shall calculate the minimal automaton by the method of residuals.

$$a^{-1}L = L \cup baA^*$$
$$b^{-1}L = L$$
$$a^{-1}(L \cup baA^*) = a^{-1}L = L \cup baA^*$$
$$b^{-1}(L \cup baA^*) = b^{-1}L \cup aA^* = L \cup aA^*$$
$$a^{-1}(L \cup aA^*) = a^{-1}L \cup A^* = A^*$$
$$b^{-1}(L \cup aA^*) = b^{-1}L = L$$
$$a^{-1}A^* = A^*$$
$$b^{-1}A^* = A^*$$

Thus the minimal automaton of L possesses four states, corresponding to the residuals $q_1 = L, q_2 = L \cup baA^*, q_3 = L \cup aA^*$ and $q_4 = A^*$.

The transitions of the minimal automaton are given in the following table.

State index	1	2	3	4
a	2	2	4	4
b	1	3	1	4

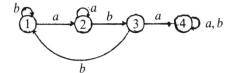

Calculation of the syntactic semigroup of L

The syntactic semigroup of L is the transition semigroup of the minimal automaton. We give first the principle of the calculation.

(1) We order the alphabet $A: a_1 < a_2 < \ldots < a_n$. We then draw up simultaneously a table of transformations and a list of relations.

(2) We calculate successively the transformations associated with words of length $1, 2, 3, \ldots$.

(3) To pass from length n to length $n + 1$, we calculate the transformations associated with words of the form $ua_i (1 \leq i \leq n)$ where u is a word of length n *appearing in the table*.

(4) Let $v = ua_i$. If the transformation associated with v does not appear in the table, we insert it. If the transformation is already associated with a word u, we write $u = v$ in the list of relations.

In our example, we shall assume $a < b$.

Length 1   The transformations associated with the words a and b are given by

	1	2	3	4
a	2	2	4	4
b	1	3	1	4

Length 2 We calculate successively (1) *aa*, (2) *ab*, (3) *ba*, (4) *bb*. The result of this calculation is given in the table below.

	1	2	3	4					Relations
							(1)		$a^2 = a$
a	2	2	4	4					
b	1	3	1	4					
(2) ab	3	3	4	4					
(3) ba	2	4	2	4					
(4) bb	1	1	1	4					

Length 3 We calculate successively (5) *aba*, (6) *abb*, (7) *baa*, (8) *bab*, (9) *bba*, (10) *bbb*. (We need not calculate *aaa* or *aab* since *aa* does not appear in the table on the left.) We notice already that *baa* = *ba* since *aa* = *a*. It will thus be unnecessary to give this relation in the list of relations. The continuation of the calculation then gives

	1	2	3	4				Relations
								$a^2 = a$
a	2	2	4	4			(10)	$b^3 = b^2$
b	1	3	1	4				
ab	3	3	4	4				
ba	2	4	2	4				
bb	1	1	1	4				
(5) aba	4	4	4	4				
(6) abb	1	1	4	4				
(8) bab	3	4	3	4				
(9) bba	2	2	2	4				

Length 4 We calculate successively (11) *abaa*, (12) *abab*, (13) *abba*, (14) *abbb*, (15) *baba*, (16) *babb*, (17) *bbaa*, (18) *bbab*.

The relations already known enable us to avoid the calculation of (11), (14) and (17) since *abaa* = *aba*, *abbb* = *abb* and *bbaa* = *bba*. Furthermore, the word *aba* is a zero of the transition semigroup (see Problem 2.7). We express this remark directly in the form *aba* = 0 in the list of relations. It is thus unnecessary to calculate (12) and (15). Then we obtain

	1	2	3	4
a	2	2	4	4
b	1	3	1	4
ab	3	3	4	4
ba	2	4	2	4
bb	1	1	1	4
aba	4	4	4	4
abb	1	1	4	4
bab	3	4	3	4
bba	2	2	2	4
babb	1	4	1	4
bbab	3	3	3	4

Relations	
(a)	$a^2 = a$
(b)	$b^3 = b^2$
(c)	$aba = 0$
(d)	$abba = a$

Length 5   We calculate successively $babba = ba$, $babbb = babb$, $bbaba = 0$, $bbabb = bb$.

Conclusion

The syntactic semigroup of L is given either by the preceding table (as a transformation semigroup) or by 'generators and relations', the relations being $a^2 = a$, $b^3 = b^2$, $aba = 0$, $abba = a$, $bbabb = bb$.

3.2.   The syntactic monoid of $L = \{a^2, aba, ba\}^*$ over the alphabet $A = \{a, b\}$

Here $L = P^*$ where P is the finite prefix code $\{a^2, aba, ba\}$, represented by the tree

To construct the minimal automaton of P^* when P is a prefix code, we proceed as follows.

(a) We attach the label 1 to the root and the leaves of the tree.

(b) We label the remaining vertices (following lexicographic order for example) observing the following rule: if the subtrees emerging from the vertices S_1 and S_2 are equal, then S_1 and S_2 have the same labels.

(c) An edge labelled by the letter a between two vertices labelled i and j corresponds to the transition $i \cdot a = j$ in the minimal automaton of P^*. If the value of $i \cdot a$ is not given by the labelled tree, we add a state 0 and we put $i \cdot a = 0$ and $0 \cdot b = 0$ for every letter b.

Example 3.1

If P is the prefix code $\{a^4, a^3ba, a^3b^2, ba^2, baba, bab^2, b^2\}$ over the alphabet $A = \{a, b\}$, the minimal automaton of P^* is given by

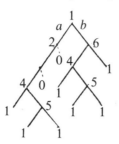

In our example, we find

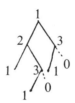

The transition monoid of this automaton can be calculated easily with the help of the algorithm described in Example 2.1. We find

	1	2	3	0
1	1	2	3	0
a	2	1	1	0
b	3	3	0	0
a^2	1	2	2	0
ab	3	3	3	0
ba	1	1	0	0
bb	0	0	0	0
aba	1	1	1	0
baa	2	2	0	0
aba^2	2	2	2	0

Relations

$$b^2 = 0$$
$$a^3 = a$$
$$a^2b = ab$$
$$(ab)^2 = ab$$
$$bab = b$$

Problems

Section 1

1.1 Show that, if $n \geq 2$, $\mathcal{T}_n$ is generated by the three functions

$$\sigma = \begin{pmatrix} 1 & 2 & \cdots & n-1 & n \\ 2 & 3 & \cdots & n & 1 \end{pmatrix}$$

$$\tau = \begin{pmatrix} 1 & 2 & 3 & \dots n \\ 2 & 1 & 3 & \dots n \end{pmatrix}$$

$$\rho = \begin{pmatrix} 1 & 2 & \dots & n-1 & n \\ 1 & 2 & \dots & n-1 & 1 \end{pmatrix}.$$

1.2. Let A, B, C be three subsets of a monoid M. Put

$$A^{-1}B = \{m \in M \mid Am \cap B \neq \varnothing\}$$
$$BC^{-1} = \{m \in M \mid mC \cap B \neq \varnothing\}$$

and

$$A^{-1}BC^{-1} = \{m \in M \mid AmC \cap B \neq \varnothing\}$$

Prove the following formulae, where N denotes a submonoid of M:

(a) $(AB)^{-1}C = B^{-1}(A^{-1}C)$ and $A(BC)^{-1} = (AC^{-1})B^{-1}$
(b) $(A^{-1}B)C^{-1} = A^{-1}BC^{-1} = A^{-1}(BC^{-1})$
(c) if $A \subset B$ then $C^{-1}A \subset C^{-1}B$ and $A^{-1}C \subset B^{-1}C$
(d) $(N^{-1}N)^{-1}N = N^{-1}N = (N^{-1}N)N$
(e) $AN \cap BN^{-1} \subset (A \cap BN^{-1})N$ and $NA \cap N^{-1}B \subset N(A \cap N^{-1}B)$

1.3 Let $\varphi : S \to T$ be a semigroup morphism. Show that if S' is a subsemigroup of S, $S'\varphi$ is a subsemigroup of T. If T' is a subsemigroup of T, $T'\varphi^{-1}$ is a subsemigroup of S.

1.4 Show that a semigroup S possesses at most one zero.

1.5 (I. Simon)   Let S be a semigroup which is finitely generated (i.e. generated by a finite set). Show that if $S \setminus E(S)$ is finite, then S is finite.

Section 2

2.1 Calculate the minimal automaton of the following languages:
(a) $L = \{ab\}$ over the alphabet $A = \{a, b\}$
(b) $L = A^*a$ over the alphabet $A = \{a, b\}$
(c) $L = A^*abA^*$ over the alphabet $A = \{a, b\}$
(d) $L = A^*abA^*$ over the alphabet $A = \{a, b, c\}$
(e) $L = (ab)^*$ over the alphabet $A = \{a, b\}$
(f) $L = A^*a^2A^*$ over the alphabet $A = \{a, b\}$

2.2 Calculate the syntactic semigroups of the languages (a)–(f).

2.3 Let L be a recognizable language and $S(L)$ be the syntactic semigroup of L. A word u of A^* is called **completable** in L if there exists $u_1, u_2 \in A^*$ such that $u_1 u u_2 \in L$. L is **dense** if every word of A^* is completable in L; otherwise it is non-dense. Show that if L is non-dense, $S(L)$ possesses a zero (which is the common syntactic image of non-completable words).

2.4 A recognizable language L is called **complete** if L^+ is dense. Let $\eta : A^+ \to S = S(L^+)$ be the syntactic morphism of L^+.

(a) Show that, if L is incomplete, S admits a *unique* 0-minimal ideal.

(b) Show that if L is complete (incomplete) the semigroup $L^+\eta$ contains an idempotent of the minimal (0-minimal) ideal of S.

2.5   Let S be a semigroup and P a subset of S. We say that P is **disjunctive** if $\sim_P$ is an equality (i.e. if $u \sim_P v$ implies $u = v$). Show that a semigroup is a syntactic semigroup (i.e. the syntactic semigroup of a language) if and only if it contains a disjunctive subset.

2.6   Give an example of a finite semigroup which is not a syntactic semigroup. Show by an example that the product of two syntactic semigroups is not necessarily syntactic.

2.7   Let $\mathscr{A} = (Q, A, \cdot)$ be a finite automaton and let S be its transition semigroup. We say that a state $q_0 \in Q$ is a **sink** of the automaton if $q_0 \cdot a = q_0$ for all $a \in A$. Show that, if an element u of S is such that, for all $q \in Q, q \cdot u = q_0$, then u is a zero of S.

Chapter 2

Varieties

The object of this chapter is to prove Eilenberg's variety theorem. This theorem establishes the existence of a one-to-one correspondence between certain classes of finite monoids, the varieties of monoids and certain classes of recognizable languages, called varieties of languages. It allows a classification of recognizable languages through the properties of their syntactic monoids.

The varieties of finite monoids are defined in the first section. It is shown that the varieties can be 'ultimately' defined by a sequence of equations (hence the name 'varieties', by analogy with algebraic varieties). The second section is devoted to the proof of the theorem on varieties and some classical examples of varieties are assembled in the final section.

1. Varieties of semigroups and monoids

1.1. Definitions and examples

All the semigroups and monoids considered in this chapter are finite. The definition of a variety of semigroups (or monoids) is due to Eilenberg (1976). It was inspired by the general definition of a variety of universal algebras given by Birkhoff, but Eilenberg's definition permits only finite products.

Definition 1.1

A variety of semigroups (or monoids) is a class of semigroups (or monoids) closed under division and under finite products.

Equivalently a class V of semigroups is a variety if V satisfies the following three conditions:

(a) if $S \in V$ and if T is a subsemigroup of S, then $T \in V$
(b) if $S \in V$ and if T is a quotient of S, then $T \in V$
(c) if $(S_i)_{i \in I}$ is a finite family of elements of V,

$$\prod_{i \in I} S_i \in V$$

This definition is not quite that of Eilenberg. In fact, we allow the empty product in our definition; consequently, the semigroup

$$1 = \prod_{i \in \emptyset} S_i$$

is an element of every variety of semigroups or of monoids. This convention allows us to simplify certain statements.

Varieties will generally be denoted by bold italic, e.g. V, W.

We give immediately some examples of varieties.

Example 1.1

The trivial variety of semigroups is the variety $T = \{\emptyset, 1\}$. It is the smallest variety of semigroups; in other words every variety of semigroups contains T. The trivial variety of monoids, consisting of the single monoid 1, is denoted by I.

Example 1.2

Every variety of semigroups (or monoids) is contained within the variety S (or M) consisting of all the finite semigroups (or monoids).

Example 1.3

We denote by G the variety of groups. We shall first verify that this is indeed a variety of monoids. The only difficulty is to verify condition (a) above. Let M be a submonoid of a group G. If $x \in M$, $x^n \in M$ for all $n > 0$. From Chapter 1, Corollary 1.7, there exists n such that x^n is idempotent and thus necessarily $x^n = 1$. It follows from this that every element of M has an inverse in M and M is indeed a subgroup of G.

Example 1.4

We denote by Com the variety of commutative monoids and by $G\mathrm{com}$ the variety (of monoids) of commutative groups.

The intersection of any family of varieties is again a variety. In particular, if C is a set of (finite) semigroups, the intersection of all the varieties containing C is a variety, called the variety generated by C and denoted by (C). The variety (C) can also be defined constructively:

$$(C) = \{S | \exists n \geq 0, \exists S_1, \ldots, S_n \in C, S < S_1 \times \ldots \times S_n\}$$

The equivalence of the two definitions is left as an exercise for the reader.

If $C = \{S\}$, we write simply (S) for the variety generated by C and we say also that (S) is the variety generated by S. If V is a variety of monoids, we denote by $(V)_S$ the variety of semigroups generated by V.

1.2. Equations of a variety

Let Σ^+ be the free semigroup over a denumerable alphabet Σ and let $u, v \in \Sigma^+$. We say that a semigroup S satisfies the equation $u = v$ if and only if $u\varphi = v\varphi$ for every morphism $\varphi: \Sigma^+ \to S$. Intuitively, this means that, if we substitute arbitrary elements of S for the letters u and v, we arrive at an equality in S. For example, S is commutative if and only if it satisfies the equation $xy = yx$; S is idempotent if and only if it satisfies the equation $x = x^2$.

We can easily show that the class of semigroups S satisfying the equation $u = v$ is a variety, denoted by $V(u, v)$.

Let $(u_n, v_n)_{n > 0}$ be a sequence of pairs of words of Σ^+. Consider the following varieties:

$$V_n = V(u_n, v_n)$$

$$V' = \bigcap_{n > 0} V_n$$

and

$$V'' = \lim V_n = \bigcup_{m > 0} \bigcap_{n \geq m} V_n$$

We say that V' and V'' are **defined** and **ultimately defined** respectively by the equations $u_n = v_n (n > 0)$; this corresponds to the fact that a semigroup is in V' or V'' if and only if it satisfies the equations $u_n = v_n$ for every $n > 0$ or for every n sufficiently large respectively.

If we replace Σ^+ by Σ^* and semigroup by monoid we can adapt everything above without difficulty to varieties of monoids. Eilenberg and Schützenberger (1975) have proved the following result.

Theorem 1.1
Every variety of semigroups (or monoids) is ultimately defined by a sequence of equations.

The proof of this theorem depends on a lemma which is interesting in itself.

Lemma 1.2
Let A be a finite alphabet and $\sim$ be a congruence with finite index over A^*. Then $\sim$ is finitely generated, i.e. there exists a finite set $F \subset A^* \times A^*$ such that $\sim$ is the smallest congruence satisfying $u \sim v$ for every $(u, v) \in F$.

Proof
If C is an equivalence class of $\sim$, we denote by $k(C)$ the length of the shortest word or words of C. Since $\sim$ has finite index, the integer $k = 1 + \max \{k(C) | C$ a class of $\sim\}$ is finite and each class of $\sim$ contains a word of length strictly smaller than k. Put

$$F = \{(u, v) \in A^* \times A^* | u \sim v, |u| \leq k, |v| < k\}$$

and let $\equiv$ be the congruence generated by F. It is clear that $u \equiv v$ implies $u \sim v$. If the converse is not true, we can find two words u and v such that $u \sim v$ and $u \not\equiv v$. Let us choose such a pair (u, v) with $|u| + |v|$ minimal. If $|u| \geq k$, then $u = xu'$ with $|u'| = k$. According to the definition of F and the choice of k, there exists $v' \in A^*$ such that $|v'| < k$ and $(u', v') \in F$. We then have $u' \equiv v'$ where $u \equiv xu' \equiv xv'$, and it follows from this that $xv' \sim v$ and $xv' \not\equiv v$; since $|xv'| < |u|$, this contradicts the minimality of $|u| + |v|$. Thus $|u| < k$ and an identical argument shows that $|v| < k$. Since $u \sim v$, it follows that $(u, v) \in F$ and therefore $u \equiv v$. This is a contradiction.

Proof of Theorem 1.1

We give the proof for a variety of monoids V. The proof can be adapted without difficulty to varieties of semigroups. $\Sigma = \{a_k | k > 0\}$ designates a denumerable alphabet, and we denote by Σ_n the alphabet $\{a_1, \ldots, a_n\}$. Since all the monoids of V are finite, we can enumerate the elements of $V: M_1, \ldots, M_n, \ldots$. For each $n > 0$, consider the monoid $S_n = M \times \ldots \times M_n$ and let $\sim_n$ be the congruence defined by

$$u \sim_n v \text{ if and only if, for every morphism } \varphi: \Sigma_n^* \to S_n, u\varphi = v\varphi$$

Since S_n and Σ_n are finite, there is only a finite number N of morphisms from Σ_n^* into S_n and $\sim_n$ has finite index. Moreover, $\Sigma_n^*/\sim_n$ is a submonoid of the product of N copies of S_n (see Chapter 1, Proposition 1.3). From the lemma, $\sim_n$ is generated by a *finite* set $E_n \subset \Sigma_n^* \times \Sigma_n^* \subset \Sigma^* \times \Sigma^*$. We shall show that

$$E = \bigcup_{n > 0} E_n$$

is a set of equations ultimately defining V.

If $M \in V$, there exists k such that M divides S_n for every $n \geq k$. Since S_n satisfies the equations E_n by construction, M satisfies E_n for every $n \geq k$.

Conversely, suppose that M satisfies E_n for every $n \geq k$. In particular, let us choose $n \geq \max(k, \text{card}(M))$ and let $\varphi: \Sigma_n^* \to M$ be a surjective morphism. By definition $u\varphi = v\varphi$ for every $(u, v) \in E_n$ and, since E_n generates $\sim_n$, we have that $u \sim_n v$ implies $u\varphi = v\varphi$. According to Chapter 1, Proposition 1.4, there exists a surjective morphism

$$\Pi: \Sigma_n^*/\sim_n \to M$$

Now, as we have seen, $\Sigma_n^*/\sim_n$ divides a direct product of copies of S_n. We can deduce from this that $\Sigma_n^*/\sim_n \in V$ and finally that $M \in V$.

In the case of a variety generated by a single monoid, we can make the preceding result more precise.

Corollary 1.3

Every variety of semigroups (monoids) generated by a single semigroup (monoid) is defined by a sequence of equations.

Proof

Suppose that $V = (M)$ and let $(u_n, v_n)_{n > 0}$ be a sequence of equations ultimately defining V. Then there exists $k > 0$ such that M satisfies $u_n = v_n$ for every $n \geq k$. It is then the same for every monoid N in V. Conversely let N satisfy $u_n = v_n$ for every $n \geq k$. Then $N \in V$. Thus V is defined by the sequence of equations $(u_n, v_n)_{n \geq k}$.

Let S be a semigroup. We call the exponent of S an integer k such that s^k is idempotent for every $s \in S$. Since S is finite, such an integer always exists.

If n is a positive integer, we denote by $\bar{n}$ the lowest common multiple of the integers $1, 2, \ldots, n$. If k is an exponent of S, we see that, for every $n \geq k$, $\bar{n}$ is also an exponent. This will enable us to define a convenient notation used by Schützenberger. Let V be a variety defined by the equations $u_n = v_n$ $(n > 0)$. We agree to replace in each equation $u_n = v_n$ all the exponents $\bar{n}$ by the symbol ω. It then follows that we can sometimes suppress the indices n totally and arrive at a unique equation. For example, the variety G is defined by the equations $x^{\bar{n}} = 1$ $(n > 0)$. With Schützenberger's convention this sequence of equations can be written simply $x^\omega = 1$.

Conversely, it is very simple to reconstruct the equations defining a variety starting from an equation using the symbol ω. Then the expression $(y^\omega x y^\omega)^\omega = y^\omega$ is an abbreviation for

$$(y^{\bar{n}} x y^{\bar{n}})^{\bar{n}} = y^{\bar{n}} \ (n > 0)$$

The advantage of this convention is that it enables us to give a direct interpretation in terms of semigroups. In fact, if x is an element of a semigroup S and if k is an exponent of S, $x^{\bar{n}}$ is equal, for every $n \geq k$, to the unique idempotent e of the subsemigroup of S generated by x. We can thus interpret ω as an exponent of the semigroup generated by x.

For example, the equation $(y^\omega x y^\omega)^\omega = y^\omega$ defines the variety LG of semigroups S such that, for every idempotent $e \in S$ and for every $x \in S$, $(exe)^\omega = e$, i.e. the semigroups S such that, for every idempotent e, eSe is a group. These semigroups are called **nil-simple**.

2. The variety theorem

Eilenberg's variety theorem enables us to give a classification of recognizable languages by means of the properties of their syntactic monoids.

If V is a variety of monoids and A is an alphabet, we denote by $A^*\mathscr{V}$ the set of (recognizable) languages of A^* whose syntactic monoid is within V. The following is an equivalent definition.

Proposition 2.1
$A^*\mathscr{V}$ is the set of languages of A^* recognized by a monoid of V.

Proof
If $L \in A^*\mathscr{V}$, then $M(L) \in V$ by definition. Now $M(L)$ recognizes L. Conversely if $L \subset A^*$ is recognized by $M \in V$, we have $M(L) < M$ and therefore $M(L) \in V$ by the definition of a variety. Thus $L \in A^*\mathscr{V}$.

Definition 2.1
A class of recognizable languages is a function $\mathscr{C}$ which associates with each alphabet A a set $A^*\mathscr{C}$ of recognizable languages of A^*.

The function $V \to \mathscr{V}$ enables us to associate with each variety of monoids a class of recognizable languages. The statement which follows show that this function is injective.

Theorem 2.2

Let V and W be two varieties of monoids. Suppose that $V \to \mathscr{V}$ and $W \to \mathscr{W}$. Then $V \subset W$ if and only if, for every finite alphabet A, $A^*\mathscr{V} \subset A^*\mathscr{W}$. In particular $V = W$ if and only if $\mathscr{V} = \mathscr{W}$.

Proof

If $V \subset W$, it follows immediately from the definitions that $A^*\mathscr{V} \subset A^*\mathscr{W}$. The converse is based on the following proposition.

Proposition 2.3

Let V be a variety of monoids and $M \in V$. Then there exist a finite alphabet A and languages $L_1, \ldots, L_k \in A^*\mathscr{V}$ such that M divides $M(L_1) \times \ldots \times M(L_k)$.

Proof

Since M is finite there exists a finite alphabet A and a surjective morphism $\varphi : A^* \to M$. For each $m \in M$, the language $L_m = m\varphi^{-1}$ is recognized by M and therefore $L_m \in A^*\mathscr{V}$. Moreover, let $\sim$ be the equivalence relation on A^* defined by $u \sim v$ if and only if, for every $m \in M$, $u \sim_{L_m} v$.

If $u \sim v$, it follows in particular that $u \sim_{L_{u\phi}} v$ whence, since $1 \cdot u \cdot 1 \in L_{u\varphi}$, $1 \cdot v \cdot 1 \in L_{u\varphi}$, i.e. $v\varphi = u\varphi$. In other words $u \sim v$ implies $u\varphi = v\varphi$ and from Chapter 1, Propositions 1.3 and 1.4, we have

$$M < \prod_{m \in M} A^*/\sim_{L_m} = \prod_{m \in M} M(L_m)$$

Completion of the proof of 2.2

Suppose that $A^*\mathscr{V} \subset A^*\mathscr{W}$ for every finite alphabet A and let $M \in V$. Then from Proposition 2.3, M divides $M(L_1) \times \ldots \times M(L_k)$ where $L_1, \ldots, L_k \in A^*\mathscr{V}$. We deduce from this that $L_1, \ldots, L_k \in A^*\mathscr{W}$, i.e. $M(L_1), \ldots, M(L_k) \in W$. Therefore $M \in W$.

It is now necessary to characterize the classes of languages which can be obtained by starting from a variety of monoids.

Definition 2.2

A variety of languages is a class of recognizable languages $\mathscr{V}$ such that

(1) for every alphabet A, $A^*\mathscr{V}$ is a boolean algebra (operations union and complementation)
(2) if $\varphi : A^* \to B^*$ is a free monoid morphism, $L \in B^*\mathscr{V}$ implies $L\varphi^{-1} \in A^*\mathscr{V}$
(3) if $L \in A^*\mathscr{V}$ and if $a \in A$, $a^{-1}L$ and $La^{-1} \in A^*\mathscr{V}$

Proposition 2.4

Let V be a variety of monoids. If $V \to \mathscr{V}$, $\mathscr{V}$ is a variety of languages.

Proof

Let L, $L_1, L_2 \in A^*\mathscr{V}$ and $a \in A$. Then by definition $M(L), M(L_1), M(L_2) \in V$. From the results of Chapter 1, we know that $A^* \backslash L$, $a^{-1}L$ and La^{-1} are recognized by $M(L)$ and that $L_1 \cup L_2$ and $L_1 \cap L_2$ are recognized by $M(L_1) \times M(L_2)$. Therefore we have $A^* \backslash L, a^{-1}L, La^{-1}, L_1 \cap L_2, L_1 \cup L_2 \in A^*\mathscr{V}$. We could give a similar proof for condition (2).

Theorem 2.5

For every variety of languages $\mathscr{V}$, there exists a variety of monoids V such that $V \to \mathscr{V}$.

Proof

Let V be the variety of monoids generated by the monoids of the form $M(L)$ where $L \in A^*\mathscr{V}$ for a certain alphabet A. Suppose that $V \to \mathscr{W}$; we shall in fact show that $\mathscr{V} = \mathscr{W}$. First, if $L \in A^*\mathscr{V}$, we have $M(L) \in V$ by definition and therefore $L \in A^*\mathscr{W}$ (still by definition). Therefore, for every alphabet A, $A^*\mathscr{V} \subset A^*\mathscr{W}$.

The inclusion $A^*\mathscr{W} \subset A^*\mathscr{V}$ is more difficult to prove. Let $L \in A^*\mathscr{W}$; then $M(L) \in V$ and therefore there exist an integer $n > 0$, alphabets A_i ($1 \le i \le n$) and languages $L_i \in A_i^*\mathscr{V}$ ($1 \le i \le n$) such that $M(L) < M(L_1) \times \ldots \times M(L_n) = M$. Let $\pi_i : M \to M(L_i)$ be the ith projection defined by $(m_1, \ldots, m_n)\pi_i = m_i$. Since $M(L)$ divides M, M recognizes L and there exists a morphism $\varphi : A^* \to M$ and a subset P of M such that $L = P\varphi^{-1}$. Finally put $\varphi_i = \varphi\pi_i$. We denote by $\eta_i : A_i^* \to M(L_i)$ the syntactic morphism of L_i ($1 \le i \le n$). Since $\eta_i : A_i^* \to M(L_i)$ is surjective, Proposition 1.9 indicates that there exists a morphism $\psi_i : A^* \to A_i^*$ such that $\varphi_i = \psi_i\eta_i$. We can summarize the situation by a diagram:

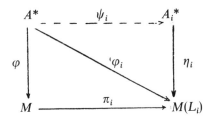

We recall that we are seeking to prove that $L \in A^*\mathscr{V}$, which is finally obtained by a succession of 'reductions' of the problem.

First stage   We have

$$L = P\varphi^{-1} = \bigcup_{m \in P} m\varphi^{-1}$$

Since $A^*\mathcal{V}$ is closed under union, it suffices to establish that for every $m \in M$ we have $m\varphi^{-1} \in A^*\mathcal{V}$.

Second stage Put $m = (m_1, \ldots, m_n)$. We have

$$m\varphi^{-1} = (m_1, \ldots, m_n)\varphi^{-1} = \bigcap_{1 \leq i \leq n} m_i \varphi_i^{-1}$$

[Detailed proof: $u \in m\varphi^{-1} \Leftrightarrow u\varphi = m = (m_1, \ldots, m_n) \Leftrightarrow$ for $1 \leq i \leq n$, $u\varphi\pi_i = m_i \Leftrightarrow$ for $1 \leq i \leq n$, $u\varphi_i = m_i \Leftrightarrow$ for $1 \leq i \leq n$, $u \in m_i\varphi_i^{-1} \Leftrightarrow u \in \bigcap_{1 \leq i \leq n} m_i\varphi_i^{-1}$.]

Since $A^*\mathcal{V}$ is closed under intersection, it suffices to establish that, for $1 \leq i \leq n$, $m_i\varphi_i^{-1} \in A^*\mathcal{V}$.

Third stage $\varphi_i = \psi_i \eta_i$ and therefore $m_i\varphi_i^{-1} = (m_i\eta_i^{-1})\psi_i^{-1}$. Since $\psi_i : A^* \to A_i^*$ is a morphism of free monoids, it suffices to prove that $m_i\eta_i^{-1} \in A_i^*\mathcal{V}$, which results from the following lemma.

Lemma 2.6

ᵧ Let $\mathcal{V}$ be a variety of languages, A a finite alphabet and $L \in A^*\mathcal{V}$. Let $\eta : A^* \to M(L)$ be the syntactic morphism of L. Then for every $m \in M(L)$, $m\eta^{-1} \in A^*\mathcal{V}$.

Proof

If $w \in A^*$, we denote by $C(w)$ the set of contexts of w in L:

$$C(w) = \{(u, v) \in A^* \times A^* \mid uwv \in L\} = \{(u, v) \in A^* \times A^* \mid w \in u^{-1}Lv^{-1}\}$$

By definition of the syntactic congruence $\sim_L$ we have

$$w \sim_L w' \text{ if and only if } C(w) = C(w')$$

Consequently the syntactic class of w, i.e. the language $w\eta\eta^{-1}$, is the set

$$\bigcap_{(u,v) \in C(w)} u^{-1}Lv^{-1} \setminus \bigcup_{(u,v) \notin C(w)} u^{-1}Lv^{-1}$$

Since $L \in A^*\mathcal{V}$ and a variety of languages is closed under right or left quotient by letters, we can easily show by induction that $u^{-1}Lv^{-1} \in A^*\mathcal{V}$ for all $u, v \in A^*$. Moreover, since L is recognizable there are finitely many residuals of the form $u^{-1}Lv^{-1}$ and the intersections and unions used in the formula above, which are apparently infinite, are in fact finite. Since $A^*\mathcal{V}$ is closed under boolean operations, we have $w\eta\eta^{-1} \in A^*\mathcal{V}$ for every $w \in A^*$ and therefore $m\eta^{-1} \in A^*\mathcal{V}$ by choosing w such that $w\eta = m$. This concludes the proof of the lemma.

In conclusion, we have proved the 'variety theorem'.

Theorem 2.7

The function $V \to \mathcal{V}$ defines a bijection between the varieties of monoids and the varieties of languages.

We can give a 'semigroup' version of this theorem. For this we define languages as subsets of a free semigroup A^+. This syntactic semigroup of L is the quotient of A^+ by the syntactic congruence $\sim_L$ (defined by $u \sim_L v$ if and only if, for every $x, y \in A^*$, $xuy \in L \Leftrightarrow xvy \in L$). The other definitions and propositions can be adapted for this case word for word if we replace the symbol $*$ by $+$ and the word monoid by semigroup. To distinguish the two types of variety of languages with which we are concerned now, we speak of $*$-variety or $+$-variety as the case may be. The most important difference between $*$-varieties and $+$-varieties is the following: a $*$-variety is closed under inverse morphism between free monoids, whereas a $+$-variety is closed under inverse morphism between free semigroups. In particular, we can use morphisms 'which erase' in the first case, i.e. morphisms applying certain letters to the empty word. This is impossible in the second case.

3. Examples of varieties

Let M be the variety of all monoids. The $*$-variety of languages which corresponds to it is the variety Rat of rational languages; this is the celebrated theorem of Kleene.

Let I be the trivial variety of monoids. The corresponding variety of languages is $\mathcal{V}$, defined by $A^*\mathcal{V} = \{\varnothing, A^*\}$ for every alphabet A.

We shall now study a very important variety of semigroups, the variety of nilpotent semigroups.

Definition 3.1
A semigroup S is **nilpotent** if for every $e \in E(S)$ and every $s \in S$ we have $es = e = se$.

There follow three other characterizations of nilpotent semigroups.

Proposition 3.1
Let S be a non-empty semigroup. The following conditions are equivalent:

(1) S is nilpotent
(2) S possesses a zero which is the only idempotent of S
(3) S possesses a zero 0 and there exists n such that $S^n = 0$
(4) there exists $n > 0$ such that S satisfies the equation $x_1 \ldots x_n = y_1 \ldots y_n$

Proof
(1) implies (2)   Since S is non-empty, it contains an idempotent e. Since $es = e = se$ for every $s \in S$, e is a zero of S. Now a semigroup can contain only one zero, for if e' is another zero we find that $ee' = e'$ and $ee' = e$.

(2) implies (3)   Denote by 0 the zero of S and let $n = \text{card}(S)$. Then (see Chapter 1) $S^n = SE(S)S = S \cdot 0 \cdot S = 0$.

(3) implies (4)   This is immediate.

(4) implies (1)   Let $s \in S$ and $e \in E(S)$. Taking $x_1 = s$ and $x_2 = \ldots = x_n = y_1$ $= \ldots = y_n = e$, we find that $s = e$ if $n = 1$ and $se = e$ if $n \geq 2$ and therefore $se = e$ in all cases. Similarly $es = e$, and consequently S is nilpotent.

Corollary 3.2
The variety **Nil** of nilpotent semigroups is ultimately defined by the equations $x_1 \ldots x_n = y_1 \ldots y_n (n > 0)$.

The following is a description of the $+$-variety of languages $\mathcal{N}$il corresponding to **Nil**.

Theorem 3.3
For every alphabet A, $A^+ \mathcal{N}$il is the set of finite or cofinite languages of A^+.

We define a language $L \subset A^+$ as cofinite if $A^+ \setminus L$ is finite.

Proof
Let L be a finite language, $\eta: A^+ \to S = S(L)$ be the syntactic morphism of L and n be the maximum length of words of L. All words u of length greater than n are incompletable in L (i.e. for every $x, y \in A^*, xuy \notin L$) and are therefore syntactically equivalent. We denote by 0 the common syntactic image of all these words; 0 is then a zero of S since, if $|v| > n$, then $|uv| > n$ and $|vu| > n$ and therefore $(u\eta) \cdot 0 = 0 \cdot (u\eta) = 0$ for every $u \in A^+$. Moreover, if $m > n, u_1, \ldots, u_m \in A^+$, we have $|u_1 \ldots u_m| > n$ and therefore $(u_1\eta) \ldots (u_m\eta) = 0$. Since η is surjective, $S^m = 0$ and S is nilpotent.

If L is cofinite, $A^+ \setminus L$ is finite and therefore $S(A^+ \setminus L) = S(L)$ is nilpotent.

Conversely, let $L \subset A^+$ be a language recognized by a nilpotent semigroup S. Then there exist $\varphi: A^+ \to S$ and a subset P of S such that $P\varphi^{-1} = L$. Let n be such that $S^n = 0$ and suppose that $0 \notin P$. Then if $|u| \geq n$, u can be written $u = u_1 \ldots u_n$ with $u_i \in A^+$ ($1 \leq i \leq n$) whence $u\eta = (u_1\eta) \ldots (u_n\eta) \in S^n = 0$. Therefore $u\eta = 0 \notin P$ and $u \notin L$, which shows that L is finite. If $0 \in P$, we have $0 \notin S \setminus P$ and therefore $A^+ \setminus L$ is finite by the same argument. Therefore if $L \in A^+ \mathcal{N}$il L is finite or cofinite.

By 'splitting' the definition of a nilpotent semigroup, we obtain two new varieties of semigroups.

Definition 3.2
We denote by $K(K^r)$ the variety of semigroups S such that $e = es$ ($e = se$) for all $s \in S$ and $e \in E(S)$.

The varieties K and K^r are defined by the equations $x^\omega y = x^\omega$ and $yx^\omega = x^\omega$ respectively. We now give a description of the $+$-variety of the corresponding language $\mathcal{K}$ or $\mathcal{K}^r$.

Theorem 3.4

For every alphabet A, $A^+\mathcal{K}$ (or $A^+\mathcal{K}'$) is the set of languages of the form $XA^* \cup Y$ (or $A^*X \cup Y$) where X and Y are finite languages of A^+.

Proof

We shall show that, if $L = XA^* \cup Y$ with X and Y finite, then $S(L) \in K$. Since $S(Y)$ is nilpotent and therefore an element of K, it is sufficient to establish that $S = S(XA^*)$ is in K. Let n be the maximum length of words of X and let u be a word of length greater than or equal to n. Then for every word $v \in A^*$, we have $uv \sim_{XA^*} u$. It is clear in fact that $xuvy \in XA^* \Leftrightarrow xu \in XA^* \Leftrightarrow xuy \in XA^*$. Hence we deduce that $ts = t$ for every $t \in S^n$ and for every $s \in S$, and therefore in particular $es = e$ for every $e \in E(S)$. Therefore $S \in K$.

Conversely, let L be recognized by a semigroup $S \in K$. Then there exists $\varphi: A^+ \to S$ such that $L = L\varphi\varphi^{-1}$. If $n = \text{card}(S)$, we have $S^n = SE(S)S = SE(S)$ since $e = es$ for every $s \in S$ and $e \in E(S)$. Suppose that $uv \in L$ with $|u| = n$. Then $u\varphi \in S^n = SE(S)$ and therefore $u\varphi = se$ with $s \in S$ and $e \in E(S)$. It follows from this that $(uv)\varphi = (u\varphi)(v\varphi) = se(v\varphi) = se = u\varphi$. Therefore $u \in L$ and moreover $u\varphi\varphi^{-1} = (se)\varphi^{-1} = (seS)\varphi^{-1} \supset uA^*$. Consequently $uA^* \subset L$; from this it follows that L can be written in the form $XA^* \cup Y$ where $X \subset A^n$ and Y is a set of words of length less than n.

We shall now define a variety of semigroups which plays an important role in the theory of semigroups.

Definition 3.3

We say that a semigroup S is **locally trivial** if for every $s \in S$, $e \in E(S)$, we have $ese = e$.

A word concerning the terminology: if S is a semigroup and e is an idempotent, the semigroup eSe is the largest monoid with e as an identity contained in S; it is the local semigroup associated with the idempotent e. The condition above indicates that all the local semigroups of S are trivial.

Other characterizations of locally trivial semigroups are given below.

Proposition 3.5

Let S be a non-empty semigroup. The following conditions are equivalent:

(1) S is locally trivial
(2) $E(S)$ is the minimal ideal of S
(3) we have $esf = ef$ for every $s \in S$, $e, f \in E(S)$

Moreover, if S satisfies these conditions, we have $S^n = E(S)$ for every $n \geq \text{card}(S)$.

   (1) implies (2)   Let I be the minimal ideal of S and let $s \in I$. Then for every $e \in E(S)$, we have $e = ese \in I$ since I is an ideal and therefore $E(S) \subset I$. However, if $e \in E(S)$ and $s \in S$, it follows that $(es)^2 = eses = es$ and $(se)^2 = sese = se$. Therefore $E(S)$ is a (non-empty) ideal of S contained in I and hence $E(S) = I$.

(2) implies (3) For this part of the proof we anticipate results from Chapter 3. If $e, f \in E(S)$, we have $ef, esf \in E(S)$ because $E(S)$ is an ideal. Now $E(S)$ is a simple idempotent semigroup and therefore $esf = e(esf)f = ef$ (see Chapter 3, Corollary 3.3).

(3) implies (1)   It is sufficient to take $e = f$ in condition (3). For the last point, we observe that $S^n = SE(S)S = E(S)$ since $E(S)$ is an ideal.

Definition 3.4
We denote by *LI* the variety of locally trivial semigroups.

This variety is defined by the equation $x^\omega y x^\omega = x^\omega$. For an explanation of the notation adopted, the reader should refer to Problem 1.2.

The $+$-variety of languages corresponding to *LI* is denoted by $\mathscr{L}\mathscr{I}$.

Theorem 3.6
For every alphabet A, $A^+\mathscr{L}\mathscr{I}$ is the set of languages of the form $XA^*Y \cup Z$ where X, Y and Z are finite languages of A^+. Equivalently, $A^+\mathscr{L}\mathscr{I}$ is equal to the boolean algebra generated by languages of the form uA^* and A^*u with $u \in A^+$.

Proof
Let $A^+\mathscr{B}$ be the boolean algebra generated by languages of the form uA^* and A^*u, where $u \in A^+$. $A^+\mathscr{B}$ contains finite languages since

$$\{u\} = uA^* \setminus \bigcup_{a \in A} uaA^*$$

Furthermore, $uA^*v = uA^* \cap A^*v \setminus F$ where F is the (finite) set of words of length less than $|u| + |v|$. It follows that every language of the form $XA^*Y \cup Z$ with X, Y, Z finite is in $A^+\mathscr{B}$. Now since, from Theorem 3.4, $S(uA^*)$ and $S(A^*u)$ are in *K* and K^r respectively and therefore in *LI*, we have $A^+\mathscr{B} \subset A^+\mathscr{L}\mathscr{I}$.

Conversely, suppose that $L \in A^+\mathscr{L}\mathscr{I}$, i.e. $S = S(L) \in LI$. Let $n = \text{card}(S)$ and let u be a word of L of length greater than or equal to $2n$. Then $u = xyz$ with $|x| = |z| = n$. We denote by $\eta : A^+ \to S$ the syntactic morphism. From Proposition 3.5, we have $x\eta, z\eta \in S^n = E(S)$ and therefore $u\eta = (x\eta)(y\eta)(z\eta) \in (x\eta)S(z\eta)$. Consequently it follows that $xA^+z \subset u\eta\eta^{-1} \subset L$ and hence we deduce that L is a finite union of languages of the form xA^*z and of a finite set of words of length greater than $2n$.

If V_1 and V_2 are two varieties of semigroups, we denote by $V_1 \vee V_2$ the smallest variety containing simultaneously V_1 and V_2. The existence of such a variety is clear; it is the intersection of all the varieties containing V_1 and V_2.

Corollary 3.7
We have the equality $LI = K \vee K^r$.

Proof
Since $K \subset LI$ and $K^r \subset LI$, we have $K \vee K^r \subset LI$. Furthermore, if $\mathscr{V}$ is the

+ -variety of languages corresponding to $K \vee K^r$, $A^+\mathscr{V}$ contains the languages of the form uA^* and A^*u and therefore also the boolean algebra generated by these languages, namely $A^+\mathscr{L}\mathscr{I}$. Hence we deduce that $LI \subset K \vee K^r$.

Note We can give a direct algebraic proof of this statement. (This is left as an exercise.)

When a variety V is generated by a single monoid, we have a direct description of the corresponding languages.

Proposition 3.8

Let $V = (M)$ be the variety of monoids generated by M and let $\mathscr{V}$ be the corresponding variety of languages. Then for every alphabet A, $A^*\mathscr{V}$ is the boolean algebra generated by the languages of the form $m\varphi^{-1}$ where $\varphi: A^* \to M$ is an arbitrary morphism and $m \in M$.

Proof

It is clear that $m\varphi^{-1} \in A^*\mathscr{V}$. Conversely, let $L \in A^*\mathscr{V}$. Then $M(L)$ divides $M^{(n)}$ for a certain $n > 0$ ($M^{(n)}$ denotes here the direct product of n copies of M) and therefore $M^{(n)}$ recognizes L. Therefore there exist a morphism $\varphi: A^* \to M^{(n)}$ and a subset $P \subset M^{(n)}$ such that $L = P\varphi^{-1}$. Since

$$L = P\varphi^{-1} = \bigcup_{m \in P} m\varphi^{-1}$$

it is sufficent to establish the result when $L = m\varphi^{-1}$ where $m = (m_1, \ldots, m_n)$ is an element of $M^{(n)}$. Now if we denote the ith projection by $\pi_i: M^{(n)} \to M$, we have

$$m = \bigcap_{1 \leq i \leq n} m_i \pi_i^{-1}$$

whence

$$m\varphi^{-1} = \bigcap_{1 \leq i \leq n} m_i(\varphi\pi_i)^{-1}$$

Since $m_i \in M$ and $\varphi\pi_i: A^* \to M$ is a morphism, we have established the result required.

We shall examine various applications of the preceding proposition. Let J_1 be the variety of idempotent and commutative monoids (or 'semi-lattices'). We denote by U_1 the monoid with two elements $\{1, 0\}$ given by $1\cdot 0 = 0\cdot 1 = 0\cdot 0 = 0$ and $1\cdot 1 = 1$.

Proposition 3.9

The variety J_1 is generated by the monoid U_1.

There exist several proofs of this result. We give here a proof using the equations, whose principle can be used again to prove results of the same type (see the Problems section).

Proof

Let $V = (U_1)$. By Corollary 1.3 V is defined by a sequence of equations. Since $U_1 \in J_1$, V is contained in J_1 and therefore satisfies the equations

$$xy = yx \qquad\qquad x = x^2 \qquad\qquad (1)$$

If $V \neq J_1$, we can find an equation

$$u = v \qquad\qquad (2)$$

which is satisfied by V but which cannot be deduced from Eqns (1). Let us choose such an equation with $|u| + |v|$ minimal. Then u and v contain at most one occurrence of each letter since otherwise we would be able to use Eqns (1) to obtain an equation equivalent to Eqn (2) but shorter. (For example, if $u = u_1 x u_2 x u_3$, it follows that $u = u_1 x x u_2 u_3 = u_1 x u_2 u_3$.) Let x be a letter of u. If we take $y = 1$ for every $y \neq x$ in Eqn (2) it follows that $x = x^{|v|_x}$, and as $x = 1$ is not an equation of U_1 we have $|v|_x \neq 0$. There is therefore an occurrence of x in v and the same argument shows that every letter of v has an occurrence in u; consequently u and v contain exactly the same letters. From this it follows that the equation $u = v$ can be (easily) deduced from $xy = yx$, which contradicts the hypothesis. Therefore $V = J_1$.

We denote by $\mathscr{J}_1$ the variety of languages corresponding to J_1.

Proposition 3.10

For every alphabet A, $A^* \mathscr{J}_1$ is the boolean algebra generated by the languages of the form $A^* a A^*$ where a is a letter. Equivalently, $A^* \mathscr{J}_1$ is the boolean algebra generated by the languages of the form B^* where B is a subset of A.

Proof

The equality of the two boolean algebras considered in the statement results from the formulae

$$B^* = A^* \setminus \bigcup_{a \in A \setminus B} A^* a A^* \qquad \text{and} \qquad A^* a A^* = A^* \setminus (A \setminus a)^*$$

Since $J_1 = (U_1)$, we can use Proposition 3.8 to describe $A^* \mathscr{J}_1$. Let $\varphi : A^* \to U_1$ be an arbitrary morphism and let $B = \{a \in A \mid a\varphi = 1\}$. Then it is clear that $1\varphi^{-1} = B^*$ and that $0\varphi^{-1} = A^* \setminus B^*$, which establishes the proposition.

Let us consider the variety of monoids $V = (\mathbb{Z}_n)$ generated by the cyclic group $\mathbb{Z}_n$ of order $n > 0$. An argument analogous to that used to prove Proposition 3.9 shows that V is defined by the equations $xy = yx$ and $x^n = 1$. A description of the corresponding languages is given below.

Proposition 3.11

Let $\mathscr{V}$ be the variety of languages corresponding to $V = (\mathbb{Z}_n)$. Then for every alphabet A, $A^* \mathscr{V}$ is the boolean algebra generated by the languages of the form $L(a, k) = \{u \in A^* \mid |u|_a \equiv k \bmod n\}$ where $a \in A$ and $0 \leq k < n$.

Proof

We naturally use Proposition 3.8. Let $\varphi: A^* \to \mathbb{Z}_n$ be an arbitrary morphism and g a generator of $\mathbb{Z}_n$. If we use a multiplicative notation for $\mathbb{Z}_n$ there exists for each $a \in A$ an integer n_a such that $a\varphi = g^{n_a}$ and $0 \le n_a < n$.

Fix $m \in \mathbb{Z}_n$ and put $m = g^k$ with $0 \le k < n$. Then

$$m\varphi^{-1} = \left\{ u \in A^* \,\middle|\, \sum_{a \in A} n_a |u|_a \equiv k \bmod n \right\}$$

Hence we deduce

$$m\varphi^{-1} = \bigcup \bigcap_{a \in A} L(a, k_a)$$

where the union is taken over the finite set of families $\{k_a\}_{a \in A}$ such that

$$\sum_{a \in A} n_a k_a \equiv k \bmod n$$

and $0 \le k_a \le n$ for every $a \in A$. The proposition follows from this formula.

We denote by $G\mathrm{com}$ the variety of commutative groups and by $\mathscr{G}\mathrm{com}$ the corresponding variety of languages.

Corollary 3.12

For every alphabet A, $A^*\mathscr{G}\mathrm{com}$ is the boolean algebra generated by the languages $L(a, k, n) = \{u \in A^* \mid |u|_a \equiv k \bmod n\}$ where $a \in A$ and $0 \le k < n$.

We denote by $\mathbb{Z}_{p,n}$ the cyclic monoid of period p and index n, i.e. $\mathbb{Z}_{p,n} = \{1, a, a^2, \ldots, a^{n+p-1}\}$ with $a^n = a^{n+p}$.

Lemma 3.13

$\mathbb{Z}_{p,n}$ is a submonoid of $\mathbb{Z}_{1,n} \times \mathbb{Z}_p$.

Proof

Let $\varphi: \mathbb{Z}_{p,n} \to \mathbb{Z}_{1,n} \times \mathbb{Z}_p$ be defined by $a^k\varphi = (a^{k_1}, a^{k_2})$ where $k_1 = \min(k, n)$, $k_2 \equiv k \bmod p$ and $0 \le k_2 < p$.

We can verify without too much trouble that φ is an injective morphism.

Consider the variety of monoids $V = (\mathbb{Z}_{1,n})$ generated by $\mathbb{Z}_{1,n}$. Imitating the proof of Proposition 3.9, we can show that V is defined by the equations $xy = yx$ and $x^n = x^{n+1}$. The following is a description of the variety corresponding to V.

Proposition 3.14

Let $\mathscr{V}$ be the variety of languages corresponding to $V = (\mathbb{Z}_{1,n})$. Then for every alphabet A, $A^*\mathscr{V}$ is the boolean algebra generated by the languages of the form $L(a, k) = \{u \in A^* \mid |u|_a = k\}$ where $a \in A$ and $0 \le k < n$.

Proof

We use yet again Proposition 3.8. Let $\varphi: A^* \to \mathbb{Z}_{1,n}$ be an arbitrary morphism and g a generator of $\mathbb{Z}_{1,n}$. Then for each $a \in A$ there exists an integer n_a such that $a\varphi = g^{n_a}$ and $0 \leq n_a \leq n$.

Let $g^k \in \mathbb{Z}_{1,n}$ with $0 \leq k \leq n$. Then

$$g^k\varphi^{-1} = \left\{ u \in A^* \,\middle|\, \sum_{a \in A} n_a|u|_a \equiv k \text{ threshold } n \right\}$$

where 'threshold n' denotes the congruence over $\mathbb{N}$ defined by $p \equiv q$ threshold n if and only if $p = q < n$ or $p, q \geq n$. Hence we can deduce *for $k < n$*

$$g^k\varphi^{-1} = \bigcup \bigcap_{a \in A} L(a, k_a)$$

The union is taken over the finite set of families $\{k_a\}_{a \in A}$ such that

$$\sum_{a \in A} n_a k_a = k$$

Finally for $k = n$ we have

$$g^n\varphi^{-1} = A^* \setminus \bigcup_{0 \leq k \leq n} g^k\varphi^{-1}$$

which concludes the proof.

Note that Proposition 3.10 can be deduced for $n = 1$.

Corollary 3.15

Let $\mathscr{C}$om be the variety of languages corresponding to **Com**, the variety of commutative monoids. Then for every alphabet A, $A^*\mathscr{C}$om is the boolean algebra generated by languages of the form $K(a, r) = \{u \in A^* \,|\, |u|_a = r\}$, where $r > 0$ and $a \in A$, or $L(a, k, p^n) = \{u \in A^* \,|\, |u|_a \equiv k \bmod p^n\}$, where $0 \leq k < p^n$, p is prime, $n > 0$ and $a \in A$.

Proof

Let $M \in$ **Com** and let N be the direct product of the cyclic submonoids of M. Let $\varphi : N \to M$ be the morphism which transforms each element of N into the product of its coordinates. Then φ is clearly surjective and therefore **Com** is generated by the cyclic monoids. Furthermore, by Lemma 3.13, $\mathbb{Z}_{q,n}$ divides $\mathbb{Z}_{1,n} \times \mathbb{Z}_q$. Thus **Com** is generated by the monoids of the form $\mathbb{Z}_{1,n}$ and by the cyclic groups. Finally a classical result from group theory shows that each cyclic group is the direct product of groups of order p^n where p is a prime number. It remains only to apply Propositions 3.11 and 3.14 to reach the conclusion.

Problems

Section 1

1.1 Show that a variety generated by a finite number of monoids $M_1, \ldots, M_n$ is also generated by the single monoid $M_1 \times \ldots \times M_n$.

1.2   If V is a variety of monoids, we denote by LV the class of semigroups which are locally in V, i.e. the semigroups S such that $eSe \in V$ for every $e \in E(S)$. Show that LV is a variety and that $L(LV) = LV$.

1.3   Let V be a variety of monoids ultimately defined by the equations $u_n = v_n$ $(n > 0)$. Put

$$u_n = x_{1,n} \ldots x_{p_n,n} \qquad\qquad v_n = y_{1,n} \ldots y_{q_n,n}$$

Show that LV is ultimately defined by the equations $u_n' = v_n'$ $(n > 0)$ where

$$u_n' = x^{\bar{n}} x_{1,n} x^{\bar{n}} x_{2,n} \ldots x^{\bar{n}} x_{p_n,n} x^{\bar{n}}$$
$$v_n' = x^{\bar{n}} y_{1,n} x^{\bar{n}} y_{2,n} \ldots x^{\bar{n}} y_{q_n,n}$$

and x is a new letter.

1.4 (Very difficult; S. W. Margolis)   We say that a variety of monoids V is maximal if $V \subset W \subset M$ implies $W = V$ or $W = M$. Show that there does not exist a maximal variety.

Section 3

3.1   Let Nil_k be the variety of semigroups defined by $x_1 \ldots x_k = y_1 \ldots y_k$ and let $\mathcal{N}i\ell_k$ be the corresponding $+$-variety of languages.
   (1) Show that a non-empty semigroup is in Nil_k if and only if S possesses a zero and $S^k = 0$.
   (2) Show that, for every alphabet A, $A^+ \mathcal{N}i\ell_k$ is the boolean algebra generated by languages of the form $\{u\}$ where $|u| < k$.

3.2   Let K_k be the variety of semigroups defined by $x_1 \ldots x_k y = x_1 \ldots x_k$ and let $\mathcal{K}_k$ be the corresponding $+$-variety. Show that, for every alphabet A, $A^+ \mathcal{K}_k$ is the set of all languages of the form $X A^* \cup Y$ where X and Y are subsets of A^+ formed of words of length equal to or less than k and less than k respectively.

3.3   Let LI_k be the variety of semigroups defined by $x_1 \ldots x_k y x_1 \ldots x_k = x_1 \ldots x_k$ and let $\mathcal{LI}_k$ be the corresponding $+$-variety. Show that, for every alphabet A, $A^+ \mathcal{LI}_k$ is the boolean algebra generated by languages of the form $u A^*$ and $A^* u$ where $|u| \leq k$.

3.4   Let U_2 be the monoid $\{1, a, b\}$ whose table is given below:

↗	1	a	b
1	1	a	b
a	a	a	b
b	b	a	b

Let $\mathcal{V}$ be the variety of languages corresponding to the variety of monoids (U_2).
   (1) Show that for every alphabet A, $A^* \mathcal{V}$ is the boolean algebra generated by all languages of the form $A^* a B^*$ where $a \in A$ and $B \subset A$.
   (2) Show that the variety (U_2) is defined by the equation $xyx = yx$.

(3) Hence deduce that a monoid M is in the variety (U_2) if and only if M is idempotent and $\mathcal{L}$-trivial (see Chapter 3 for definitions).

(4) Show that L is in $A^*\mathcal{V}$ if and only if L is a disjoint union of languages of the form

$$\{a_1,\ldots,a_n\}^*a_n\{a_1,\ldots,a_{n-1}\}^*\ldots a_1^*a_1$$

where the a_i are distinct letters of A.

3.5 Let $X \subset A^+$ be a complete finite biprefix code. Show that $S(X^+)$ is a nil-simple semigroup (i.e., we recall, eSe is a group for all $e \in S$). The variety $\boldsymbol{LG}$ thus contains the syntactic semigroups of languages X^+, where X is finite, complete and biprefix.

Open problem (Schützenberger): is the variety $\boldsymbol{LG}$ generated by the semigroups in question?

Chapter 3

Structure of Finite Semigroups

The object of this chapter is to present the classical theory of finite semigroups: Green's relations, the structure of regular $\mathscr{D}$-classes and the structure of the minimal ideal. We shall also give an algorithm for practical calculation illustrated by numerous examples. However, we have not incorporated in this chapter either the Schützenberger group of a $\mathscr{D}$-class or the decomposition into blocks of 0-simple semigroups, for these results will not be directly used in this book. Finally, the last section is a reminder of V-morphisms and relational morphisms, certain aspects of whose definition recalls that of transduction in language theory.

1. Green's relations

These fundamental equivalence relations were introduced and studied by Green in 1951. They are now basic in the theory of semigroups.

Let S be a semigroup. We define on S four equivalence relations $\mathscr{R}, \mathscr{L}, \mathscr{H}$ and $\mathscr{J}$ called Green's relations:

$$a \mathscr{R} b \Leftrightarrow aS^1 = bS^1$$
$$a \mathscr{L} b \Leftrightarrow S^1a = S^1b$$
$$a \mathscr{J} b \Leftrightarrow S^1aS^1 = S^1bS^1$$
$$a \mathscr{H} b \Leftrightarrow a \mathscr{R} b \text{ and } a \mathscr{L} b$$

Then $a \mathscr{R} b$ if and only if there exist $c, d \in S^1$ such that $ac = b$ and $bd = a$, $a \mathscr{L} b$ if and only if there exist $c, d \in S^1$ such that $ca = b$ and $db = a$, etc. Parallel with these equivalence relations, we can define four quasi-order relations (i.e. reflexive and transitive relations) by

$$a \leq_{\mathscr{R}} b \Leftrightarrow aS^1 \subset bS^1$$
$$a \leq_{\mathscr{L}} b \Leftrightarrow S^1a \subset S^1b$$
$$a \leq_{\mathscr{J}} b \Leftrightarrow S^1aS^1 \subset S^1bS^1$$
$$a \leq_{\mathscr{H}} b \Leftrightarrow a \leq_{\mathscr{R}} b \text{ and } a \leq_{\mathscr{L}} b$$

It is clear that if $\mathcal{K}$ denotes one of Green's relations we have $a \mathcal{K} b$ if and only if $a \leq_\mathcal{K} b$ and $b \leq_\mathcal{K} a$. Consequently, we shall use the notation $a <_\mathcal{K} b$ as an abbreviation of $a \leq_\mathcal{K} b$ and not $a \mathcal{K} b$.

Proposition 1.1

The relations $\leq_\mathcal{R}$ and $\mathcal{R}$ are left compatible with multiplication. The relations $\leq_\mathcal{L}$ and $\mathcal{L}$ are right compatible with multiplication.

Proof

If $a \leq_\mathcal{R} b$ then $aS^1 \subset bS^1$ and therefore $caS^1 \subset cbS^1$ for every $c \in S$. Therefore $ca \leq_\mathcal{R} cb$. The proofs are similar in the other cases.

The result which follows will enable us to define a fifth Green's relation, i.e. the relation $\mathcal{D}$.

Proposition 1.2

The relations $\mathcal{R}$ and $\mathcal{L}$ commute. Consequently the relation $\mathcal{D} = \mathcal{R}\mathcal{L} = \mathcal{L}\mathcal{R}$ is the smallest equivalence relation containing $\mathcal{R}$ and $\mathcal{L}$.

Proof

Suppose that $a \mathcal{L}\mathcal{R} b$. Then there exists $c \in S$ such that $a \mathcal{L} c$ and $c \mathcal{R} b$.

Therefore there exist $u, v \in S^1$ such that $a = uc$ and $b = cv$. We have $av = ucv = ub = d$. Moreover, from Proposition 1.1 $a \mathcal{L} c$ implies $d = av \mathcal{L} cv = b$ and likewise $c \mathcal{R} b$ implies $a = uc \mathcal{R} ub = d$. Therefore $a \mathcal{R} d$ and $d \mathcal{L} b$, whence $a \mathcal{R}\mathcal{L} b$. Similarly, if $a \mathcal{R}\mathcal{L} b$ then $a \mathcal{L}\mathcal{R} b$. Therefore $\mathcal{R}\mathcal{L} = \mathcal{L}\mathcal{R}$.

We can therefore give the following definition of $\mathcal{D}$:

$$a \mathcal{D} b \Leftrightarrow \exists c \in S \ a \mathcal{R} c \text{ and } c \mathcal{L} b \Leftrightarrow \exists c \in S \ a \mathcal{L} c \text{ and } c \mathcal{R} b$$

The result which follows is fundamental.

Proposition 1.3

In a finite semigroup S, $\mathcal{J} = \mathcal{D}$.

Proof

If $a \mathcal{D} b$ there exists c such that $a \mathcal{R} c$ and $c \mathcal{L} b$. Hence we can deduce $a \mathcal{J} c$ and $c \mathcal{J} b$, whence $a \mathcal{J} b$.

Conversely suppose that $a \mathcal{J} b$. Then there exist $u, v, x, y \in S^1$ such that $uav = b$ and $xby = a$. Hence we can deduce $(xu)a(vy) = a$, whence $(xu)^k a(vy)^k = a$ for every $k > 0$. Since S is finite, we can choose k and l such that $(xu)^k = e$ and $(vy)^l = f$ are idempotent. In this case $(xu)^{kl} a(vy)^{kl} = a = eaf$, whence $(xu)^k a = ea = e(eaf) = eaf = a = af = a(vy)^l$. Therefore $ua \mathcal{L} a$ and $av \mathcal{R} a$. The first relation implies $b = uav \mathcal{L} av$ and finally $b \mathcal{D} a$.

Proposition 1.4 summarizes some useful properties of Green's relations. From now on all semigroups are assumed to be finite. In particular $\mathcal{D} = \mathcal{J}$.

Proposition 1.4

(1) Let e be an idempotent of S. Then $a \leq_{\mathcal{R}} e$ if and only if $ea = a$ and $a \leq_{\mathcal{L}} e$ if and only if $ae = a$.

(2) $\begin{cases} \text{If } a \leq_{\mathcal{J}} ax \text{ then } a \mathcal{J} ax \text{ and } a \mathcal{R} ax. \\ \text{If } a \leq_{\mathcal{J}} xa \text{ then } a \mathcal{J} xa \text{ and } a \mathcal{L} xa. \end{cases}$

(3) $\begin{cases} \text{If } a \leq_{\mathcal{R}} axy \text{ then } a, ax \text{ and } axy \text{ are } \mathcal{R}\text{-equivalents.} \\ \text{If } a \leq_{\mathcal{L}} yxa \text{ then } a, xa \text{ and } yxa \text{ are } \mathcal{L}\text{-equivalents.} \end{cases}$

(4) $\begin{cases} \text{If } a \leq_{\mathcal{L}} b \text{ and if } a \mathcal{J} b \text{ then } a \mathcal{L} b. \\ \text{If } a \leq_{\mathcal{R}} b \text{ and if } a \mathcal{J} b \text{ then } a \mathcal{R} b. \end{cases}$

Proof
(1) If $a \leq_{\mathcal{R}} e$, there exists $u \in S^1$ such that $a = eu$. Hence we can deduce $ea = eeu = eu = a$. The converse is immediate and the proof for $a \leq_{\mathcal{L}} e$ is similar.

(2) Since $ax \leq_{\mathcal{J}} a$, we have in fact $a \mathcal{J} ax$ and there exist $u, v \in S^1$ such that $uaxv = a$, whence $u^k a(xv)^k = a$ for every $k > 0$. Let us choose k such that $e = u^k$ is idempotent. It follows that $ea(xv)^k = a$, whence $ea = eea(xv)^k = ea(xv)^k = a$. Hence we can deduce $a(xv)^k = a$ and therefore $a \mathcal{R} ax$. The proof for the case $a \leq_{\mathcal{J}} xa$ is similar.

(3) If $a \leq_{\mathcal{R}} axy$, it follows that $a \leq_{\mathcal{R}} axy \leq_{\mathcal{R}} ax \leq_{\mathcal{R}} a$, whence $a \mathcal{R} ax \mathcal{R} axy$. There is a similar proof for the relation $\mathcal{L}$.

(4) Since $a \leq_{\mathcal{L}} b$ there exists $u \in S^1$ such that $a = ub$. Hence we can deduce $ub \mathcal{J} b$ and therefore $b \leq_{\mathcal{J}} ub = a$. From (2), we have $b \mathcal{L} ub = a$.

If $a \in S$, we denote by R_a, L_a, H_a and D_a the $\mathcal{R}$-class, $\mathcal{L}$-class, $\mathcal{H}$-class and $\mathcal{D}$-class respectively containing a. We note that $H_a = R_a \cap L_a$. Let R be an $\mathcal{R}$-class and L an $\mathcal{L}$-class. We shall show that $R \cap L \neq \varnothing$ if and only if R and L are within the same $\mathcal{D}$-class. If $a \in R \cap L$, we have $R = R_a$ and $L = L_a$ and therefore R and L are contained in D_a. Conversely, if R and L are in the same $\mathcal{D}$-class of S, then for every $x \in R$ and $y \in L$ there exists $a \in S$ such that $x \mathcal{R} a$ and $a \mathcal{L} y$ (since $x \mathcal{D} y$), and therefore $a \in R \cap L$. It follows from this that we can represent a $\mathcal{D}$-class by the classical 'egg-box' picture (Fig. 1) where each cell represents an $\mathcal{H}$-class, each row

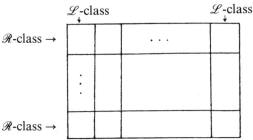

Fig. 1.

constitutes an $\mathcal{R}$-class and each column constitutes an $\mathcal{L}$-class. The possible presence of an idempotent within an $\mathcal{H}$-class is traditionally indicated by a star (Fig. 2).

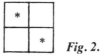

Fig. 2.

The proposition which follows is fundamental. It shows that two $\mathcal{L}$-classes (or $\mathcal{R}$-classes or $\mathcal{H}$-classes) of one and the same $\mathcal{D}$-class have the same cardinality.

Proposition 1.5 (Green's lemma)

Let $a, b \in S$ be such that $a \mathcal{R} b$. Then there exist $u, v \in S^1$ such that $au = b$ and $bv = a$. Let ρ_u and ρ_v be the right translations defined by $x\rho_u = xu$ and $x\rho_v = xv$. Then ρ_u and ρ_v induce inverse bijections from L_a onto L_b and from L_b onto L_a which preserve the $\mathcal{H}$-classes, i.e. for every $x, y \in L_a$ or L_b, $x \mathcal{H} y$ if and only if $x\rho_u \mathcal{H} y\rho_u$ or $x\rho_v \mathcal{H} y\rho_v$ respectively (Fig. 3).

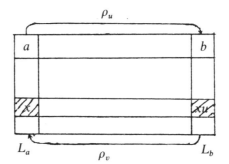

Fig. 3.

Proof

$x \mathcal{L} a$ implies $xu \mathcal{L} au = b$. Therefore ρ_u is a function from L_a into L_b. Moreover, there exists $t \in S^1$ such that $x = ta$ and therefore $x\rho_u\rho_v = xuv = tauv = tbv = ta = x$, which shows that $\rho_u\rho_v$ is the identity on L_a. We can show in the same way that ρ_v is a function from L_b onto L_a and that $\rho_v\rho_u$ is the identity on L_b, which establishes the first part of the proposition. Moreover, if $x \in L_a$, we have $xuv = x$ and therefore $x \mathcal{R} xu$. Consequently $x \mathcal{H} y$ implies $xu \mathcal{H} yu$. Likewise $xu \mathcal{H} yu$ implies $x = xuv \mathcal{H} yuv = y$.

We have of course a dual statement by considering two $\mathcal{L}$-equivalent elements.

Proposition 1.6

Let $a, b \in S$. Then $ab \in R_a \cap L_b$ if and only if $R_b \cap L_a$ contains an idempotent (Fig. 4).

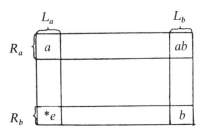

Fig. 4.

Proof

Suppose that $ab \in R_a \cap L_b$. Then by Green's lemma ρ_b induces a bijection from L_a onto L_b. Let $e \in R_b \cap L_a$ be such that $e\rho_b = eb = b$. Since $e \mathscr{R} b$ there exists $u \in S^1$ such that $e = bu$. Therefore we have $e^2 = ebu = bu = e$ and e is idempotent. Conversely if $e = e^2 \in R_b \cap L_a$, then $eb = b$ and $ae = a$ (Proposition 1.4(1)). Since $e \mathscr{R} b$ we have $a = ae \mathscr{R} ab$ and since $e \mathscr{L} a$ we have $b = eb \mathscr{L} ab$ which shows that $ab \in R_a \cap L_b$.

Corollary 1.7

Let H be an $\mathscr{H}$-class of S. The following conditions are equivalent:

(a) H contains an idempotent
(b)   there exist $a, b \in H$ such that $ab \in H$
(c) H is a maximum group in S

Proof

It is clear that (c) implies (a) and that (a) implies (b). If (b) is satisfied we have $H = R_a \cap L_b = R_b \cap L_a$ and therefore H contains an idempotent e, from Proposition 1.6. If $g, h \in H$, we have $e \in R_h \cap L_g$ and therefore, again from Proposition 1.6, $gh \in H$. Therefore H is a semigroup and even a monoid since $eg = g = ge$ for every $g \in H$ (Proposition 1.4). If $h \in H$, ρ_h is a bijection from H onto H from Green's lemma. In particular there exists h' such that $h'\rho_h = h'h = e$. Therefore H is a group. Finally every element g of a group containing e satisfies $g \mathscr{H} e$.

The following is another remarkable consequence of Green's lemma.

Proposition 1.8

Two maximal subgroups contained within one and the same $\mathscr{D}$-class of a semigroup S are isomorphic.

Proof

From Corollary 1.7, two maximal subgroups are of the form H_e, H_f with $e, f \in E(S)$. Since H_e and H_f are within the same $\mathscr{D}$-class, there exists $a \in R_e \cap L_f$. Therefore we have $ea = a$ and $a'a = f$ for a certain $a' \in S^1$. Now Green's lemma and its dual version show that the function $x \to a'xa$ is a bijection from H_e onto H_f which transforms e into $a'ea = a'a = f$.

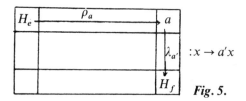

Fig. 5.

We shall see that the function $x \to a'xa$ is a morphism. We note first that $aa'aa' = afa' = aa'$ since $af = a$ from Proposition 1.4(1). Therefore aa' is an idempotent of R_a. From this it follows that $aa'z = z$ for every $z \in R_a$. In particular, if $x, y \in H_e$, $(a'xa)(a'ya) = a'x(aa'y)a = a'xya$ which establishes the result required.

An element $a \in S$ is called **regular** if there exists $s \in S$ such that $asa = a$. We say that a $\mathscr{D}$-class (or an $\mathscr{R}$-, $\mathscr{L}$- or $\mathscr{H}$-class) is regular if all its elements are regular. The proposition which follows gives various characterizations of regular $\mathscr{D}$-classes.

Proposition 1.9
Let D be a $\mathscr{D}$-class. The following conditions are equivalent.

(i) D is regular.
(ii) D contains a regular element.
(iii) Each $\mathscr{R}$-class of D contains at least one idempotent.
(iv) Each $\mathscr{L}$-class of D contains at least one idempotent.
(v) D contains at least one idempotent.
(vi) There exist $x, y \in D$ such that $xy \in D$.

Proof
If $a = asa$, then $a \mathscr{R} e$ where $e = e^2 = as$. Conversely if $a \mathscr{R} e$, where e is idempotent, there exists $u \in S^1$ such that $au = e$ and therefore $a = ea = e^2a = auea$. Likewise $a = asa$ if and only if L_a contains an idempotent.
Let a be regular and $b \in D$. Then there exists c such that $a \mathscr{R} c$ and $c \mathscr{L} b$. As a is regular $R_a = R_c$ contains an idempotent and therefore c is regular. Consequently $L_c = L_b$ contains an idempotent and b is regular. This establishes the equivalence of the first four conditions. Moreover, it is obvious that (iii) implies (v) and (v) implies (ii), and the equivalence of (v) and (vi) results from Proposition 1.6.

Let S be a subsemigroup of T. It is often useful to compare Green's relations defined in S and in T. This is the object of the following proposition.

Proposition 1.10
Let S be a subsemigroup of T and D a regular $\mathscr{D}$-class of S. Then the restrictions to D of Green's relations in S and in T coincide.

Proof
Denote by $\mathscr{R}_S$ and $\mathscr{R}_T$ Green's relations $\mathscr{R}$ in S and in T. Let $x, y \in D$ be such that

$x \mathcal{R}_T y$. Since D is a regular $\mathcal{D}$-class of S there exist $e, f \in E(S)$ such that $e \mathcal{R}_S x$ and $f \mathcal{R}_S y$. Hence we deduce that $e \mathcal{R}_T x \mathcal{R}_T y \mathcal{R}_T f$, whence from Proposition 1.4(1) $ef = f$ and $fe = e$. Consequently $e \mathcal{R}_S f$ and $x \mathcal{R}_S y$. The proof for other Green's relations is similar.

We also note the following statement.

Proposition 1.11
Let S be a subsemigroup of T. Let $x \in S$, $a, b \in S^1$ and let e be an idempotent of T. Suppose that we have *within* T $e \mathcal{R} bx$, $bx \mathcal{L} x$, $x \mathcal{R} xa$ and $xa \mathcal{L} e$. Then $e \in S$ and e, xa, bx and x are in the same (regular) $\mathcal{D}$-class of S.

Proof
The situation is summarized in Fig. 6.

x		xa
bx		e

Fig. 6.

We use the same notation as above. Since the intersection of the $\mathcal{R}_T$-class of bx and the $\mathcal{L}_T$-class of xa contains an idempotent, we have $xabx \mathcal{H}_T x$ from Proposition 1.6. By Green's lemma ρ_{abx} is a bijection of H, the $\mathcal{H}_T$-class of x. Consequently a suitable power of ρ_{abx}, say ρ_{abx}^k, induces the identity on H. In particular $x(abx)^k = x$ and since $a, b, x \in S^1$ it follows that $xa \mathcal{R}_S x$, $x \mathcal{L}_S bx$ and $xabx \mathcal{H}_S x$. By Proposition 1.6 the intersection of the $\mathcal{R}_S$-class of bx and the $\mathcal{L}_S$-class of xa contains an idempotent which is necessarily e (for it is contained within the $\mathcal{H}_T$-class of e and an $\mathcal{H}$-class contains at most one idempotent). Consequently $e \in S$ and $e \mathcal{L}_S xa$, $xa \mathcal{R}_S x$ imply $e \mathcal{D}_S x$.

We say that two elements a and b of a semigroup S are **conjugate** if there exists $u, v \in S$ such that $a = uv$ and $b = vu$. The proposition which follows gives an important characterization of conjugate idempotents.

Proposition 1.12
Let e and f be two idempotents of S. Then $e \mathcal{D} f$ if and only if e and f are conjugate.

Proof
Suppose first that there exist $u, v \in S$ with $e = uv$ and $f = vu$. Then we have $uvuv = uv$ and $vuvu = vu$, whence $uv \mathcal{R} uvu$ and $uvu \mathcal{L} vu$. Hence we deduce that $e = uv \mathcal{D} vu = f$.
Conversely suppose that $e \mathcal{D} f$. Then there exist $a, b \in S$ such that $e \mathcal{R} a$, $a \mathcal{L} f$, $e \mathcal{L} b$ and $b \mathcal{R} f$. By Proposition 1.6 we have $ab \mathcal{H} e$ and $ba \mathcal{H} f$ and by

Corollary 1.7 there exists an integer $n > 0$ such that $(ab)^n = e$ and $(ba)^n = f$. If we put $u = a$ and $v = b(ab)^{n-1}$, we find that $uv = e$ and $vu = f$.

2. Practical calculation

In practice, at least in the theory of languages, the semigroups are given as semigroups of transformations. We shall therefore begin by examining Green's relations in the semigroup $\mathcal{T}(E)$ of functions from E into E. If $a \in \mathcal{T}(E)$ we denote by Im a the image of a and by Ker a the partition induced by the equivalence relation $\sim$ over E defined by $x \sim y \Leftrightarrow xa = ya$. The rank of a is the integer rg a = card(Im a) = card(Ker a) and Ker a is called the **kernel** of a. For example if a is given by

$$a = \begin{pmatrix} 1 & 2 & 3 & 4 & 5 & 6 & 7 \\ 1 & 3 & 2 & 2 & 2 & 3 & 1 \end{pmatrix}$$

we have Im $a = \{1, 2, 3\}$, Ker $a = 17/26/345$ and rg $a = 3$.

Proposition 2.1
Let $a, b \in \mathcal{T}(E)$. Then

(1) $a \leq_{\mathcal{R}} b$ if and only if Ker a is a partition coarser than Ker b and $a \mathcal{R} b$ if and only if Ker a = Ker b
(2) $a \leq_{\mathcal{L}} b$ if and only if Im $a \subset$ Im b and $a \mathcal{L} b$ if and only if Im a = Im b
(3) $a \leq_{\mathcal{J}} b$ if and only if rg $a \leq$ rg b and $a \mathcal{J} b$ if and only if rg a = rg b.

Proof
(1) If $a \leq_{\mathcal{R}} b$, there exists $u \in \mathcal{T}(E)$ such that $a = bu$ and therefore Ker a is coarser than Ker b. Conversely, if this condition is satisfied, $q_1 b = q_2 b$ implies $q_1 a = q_2 a$; it follows from this that the relation $u = b^{-1}a$ is in fact a function from E into E such that $bu = a$. Therefore $a \leq_{\mathcal{R}} b$.
(2) If $a \leq_{\mathcal{L}} b$, there exists $u \in \mathcal{T}(E)$ such that $a = ub$ and therefore Im $a \subset$ Im b. Conversely, if Im $a \subset$ Im b, for every $q \in E$ we have $qa \in$ Im $a \subset$ Im b and there exists an element $q' \in E$ such that $q'b = qa$. If we put $q' = qu$, it follows that $qub = qa$ for all $q \in E$, i.e. $ub = a$. Therefore $a \leq_{\mathcal{L}} b$.
(3) If $a \leq_{\mathcal{J}} b$, there exist $u, v \in \mathcal{T}(E)$ such that $a = ubv$ and therefore rg $a \leq$ rg b. We construct a function $u: E \to E$ by sending each class of Ker a onto an element of Im b and two distinct classes onto two distinct elements; this is possible since card(Im a) = card(Ker a) $\leq$ card(Im b). Then Ker u = Ker a and Im $u \subset$ Im b by construction. Therefore $a \mathcal{R} u$ and $u \leq_{\mathcal{L}} b$ from (1) and (2), and finally $a \leq_{\mathcal{J}} u \leq_{\mathcal{J}} b$.

We can now pass to the general study of transformation semigroups. Given a set E and a partition $\mathscr{E} = \{E_1, \dots, E_n\}$ of E, we say that F is a **transversal** of $\mathscr{E}$ if, for $1 \leq i \leq n$, card($E_i \cap F$) = 1.

Proposition 2.2

Let S be a subsemigroup of $\mathcal{T}(E)$. An element a belongs to a group within S if and only if Im a is a transversal of Ker a.

Proof

If a is within a group of S, $a^n = a$ for a certain $n \geq 2$ and therefore a induces a bijection on Im a. Let K be a class of Ker a. If card$(K \cap $ Im $a) \geq 2$, two elements of Im a have the same image under a, which contradicts the above. Therefore card$(K \cap $ Im $a) \leq 1$ for every $K \in $ Ker a. Furthermore, if $K \cap $ Im $a = \varnothing$ for a class K of Ker a, it follows that

$$\text{card}(\text{Im } a) = \sum_{E \in \text{Ker} a} \text{card}(K \cap \text{Im } a) < \text{card}(\text{Ker } a)$$

a contradiction. Therefore Im a is a transversal of Ker a.

Conversely, if this condition is satisfied, a induces a bijection on its image and therefore $a^n = a$ for a certain $n \geq 2$. Therefore a is within a group of S, from Chapter 1, Proposition 1.6.

Part of Proposition 2.1 extends to all the transformation semigroups.

Proposition 2.3

Let S be a subsemigroup of $\mathcal{T}(E)$ and $a, b \in S$. Then

(1) if $a \leq_{\mathcal{R}} b$, Ker a is a coarser partition than Ker b, and if $a \mathcal{R} b$, Ker $a = $ Ker b
(2) if $a \leq_{\mathcal{L}} b$, Im $a \subset $ Im b, and if $a \mathcal{L} b$, Im $a = $ Im b
(3) if $a \leq_{\mathcal{J}} b$, rg $a \leq $ rg b, and if $a \mathcal{J} b$, rg $a = $ rg b

Proof
See Proposition 2.1.

Proposition 2.2 enables us to locate very easily the elements of a group in S. We can then reconstruct completely the $\mathcal{D}$-class of such an element x with the help of the following algorithm.

(1) We calculate all the images of the form Im xr (where $r \in S^1$) such that card(Im xr) = card(Im x). For each image I thus obtained we retain the value of an r such that Im $xr = I$.

[Note that it is not necessary to know all the elements of S^1 to make this calculation. In fact it is sufficient to calculate Ia where a is a generator of S and I = Im xr is an image of the list of images; if card$(Ia) < $ card I, or if Ia already appears in the list, we pass to the following generator (and then to the following image).]

(2) Parallel to operation (1) we calculate all the transformations of the form xr ($r \in S^1$) such that Im $xr = $ Im x. We obtain a set H of elements of S which is the $\mathcal{H}$-class of x.

(3) We calculate all the partitions of the form $\text{Ker } sx$ (where $s \in S^1$) such that $\text{card}(\text{Ker } sx) = \text{card}(\text{Ker } x)$. For each partition K thus obtained, we retain the value of an s such that $K = \text{Ker } sx$.

(4) Among the images calculated in (1), we retain only those which are transversals of one of the partitions calculated in (3): we obtain a set $\mathscr{I} = \{\text{Im } xr_1, \ldots, \text{Im } xr_n\}$ (where $r_1 = 1$). Moreover, among the partitions calculated in (3), we retain only those which admit as a transversal one of the images calculated in (1): we obtain a set $\mathscr{K} = \{\text{Ker } s_1 x, \ldots, \text{Ker } s_m x\}$ (where $s_1 = 1$).

	$\text{Im } xr_1$		$\text{Im } xr_j$		$\text{Im } xr_n$
$\text{Ker } x = \text{Ker } s_1 x$	H		xr_j		
$\text{Ker } s_i x$	$s_i x$		H_{ij}		
$\text{Ker } s_m x$	$s_m x$				

Fig. 7.

(5) The results are summarized in a double-entry table (Fig. 7). The diagram obtained is the 'egg-box' picture of the $\mathscr{D}$-class of x. If $H_{ij} = R_{s_i x} \cap L_{xr_j}$, we have $H_{ij} = s_i H r_j$ which enables us to calculate the $\mathscr{D}$-class completely. Finally the $\mathscr{H}$-class H_{ij} is a group if and only if $\text{Im } xr_j$ is a transversal of $\text{Ker } s_i x$.

Justification of the algorithm

We recall that S is a subsemigroup of $\mathscr{T}(E)$ and that x is an element of a group within S. Suppose that xr is in R_x and that $e \in E(S)$ and $s \in S$ are such that $x \mathscr{R} xr$, $xr \mathscr{L} e$, $e \mathscr{R} sx$ and $sx \mathscr{L} x$ (Fig. 8).

	x		xr
	sx		e

Fig. 8.

Then by Proposition 2.2 Im e is a transversal of Ker e and by Proposition 2.3 Im $e =$ Im xr and Ker $sx =$ Ker e, so that Im xr is a transversal of Ker sx. Conversely, suppose that Im xr is a transversal of a certain Ker sx (where card(Im xr) = card(Im x) and card(Ker sx) = card(Ker x)). Let $e \in \mathcal{T}(E)$ be a transformation with image Im xr and with kernel Ker sx. (Exercise: convince yourself of the existence of e.) Then by Proposition 2.1 we have *within* $\mathcal{T}(E)$ $x \mathcal{D} xr \mathcal{D} sx$, $xr \mathcal{L} e$ and $e \mathcal{R} sx$. From this we can deduce $x \mathcal{R} xr$, $xr \mathcal{L} e$, $e \mathcal{R} sx$ and $sx \mathcal{L} x$. However, $x, xr, sx \in S$ and by Proposition 1.11 we have $e \in S$, and x, xr, sx and e are in the same $\mathcal{D}$-class of S.

The above shows that R_x is actually calculated by the preceding algorithm. The proof is similar for L_x. Finally, the other $\mathcal{R}$-classes and $\mathcal{L}$-classes are obtained with the help of Green's lemma.

Example 2.1   Syntactic semigroup of the language $c^*ab\{b, c\}^*$ over the alphabet $\{a, b, c\}$

The minimal automaton is

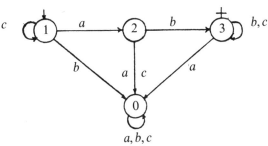

	1	2	3	0
a	2	0	0	0
$*b$	0	3	3	0
$*c$	1	0	3	0
$*0 = a^2$	0	0	0	0
ab	3	0	0	0
$*cb$	0	0	3	0

013
02/1/3 | $\overset{*}{c}$ |

02
1/023 | a |

03
1/023 | ab |

03
01/23 | $\overset{*b}{*cb}$ |

| $\overset{1}{*0}$ |

Example 2.2

Let S be the semigroup

	1	2	3	4	5	6	7	8
a	6	8	6	8	2	4	2	4
b	3	3	4	4	7	7	8	8
$*a^2$	4	4	4	4	8	8	8	8
ab	7	8	7	8	3	4	3	4
ba	6	6	8	8	2	2	4	4
a^3	8	8	8	8	4	4	4	4
aba	2	4	2	4	6	8	6	8
bab	7	7	8	8	3	3	4	4
$*abab$	3	4	3	4	7	8	7	8
$*baba$	2	2	4	4	6	6	8	8

<u>Relations</u>

$$b^2 = a^2$$
$$a^2b = a^2$$
$$ab^2 = a^3$$
$$ba^2 = a^2$$
$$a^4 = a^2$$
$$ababa = a$$
$$babab = b$$

	3478	2468
13/24/57/68	ab / $*abab$	a / aba
12/34/56/78	bab / b	ba / $*baba$

	48
1234/5678	$* a^2$ / a^3

Example 2.3 $\mathscr{T}_3$

	1	2	3
a	2	3	1
b	2	1	3
$c^2 = c$	1	2	1
a^2	3	1	2
$1 = a^3$	1	2	3
ab	1	3	2
ac	2	1	1
ba	3	2	1
$ac = bc$	2	1	1
ca	2	3	2
cb	2	1	2
$ba = a^2b$	3	2	1
a^2c	1	1	2
$a^2c = abc$	1	1	2
aca	3	2	2
acb	1	2	2

	1	2	3
ca^2	3	1	3
cab	1	3	1
$cb = cac$	2	1	2
cba	3	2	3
a^2ca	2	2	3
a^2cb	2	2	1
aca^2	1	3	3
$acab$	3	1	1
$acba$	2	3	3
$cba = ca^2b$	3	2	3
ca^2c	1	1	1
a^2ca^2	3	3	1
a^2cab	1	1	3
a^2cba	3	3	2
$ca^2cb = ca^2ca$	2	2	2
ca^2ca^2	3	3	3

Relations

$a^3 = 1$ $\quad b^2 = 1$ $\quad c^2 = c$ $\quad ba = a^2b$ $\quad ba^2 = ab$ $\quad bab = a^2$
$aba = b$ $\qquad a^2c = abc$ $\quad ac = bc$
$bac = c$ $\qquad cb = cac$ $\quad cba = ca^2b$

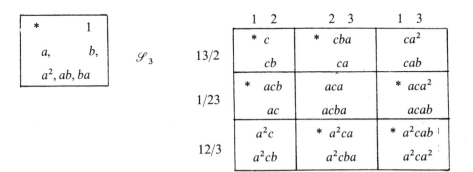

*	1
a,	b,
a^2, ab, ba	

$\mathscr{S}_3$

		1 2	2 3	1 3
13/2		* c cb	* cba ca	ca^2 cab
1/23		* acb ac	aca $acba$	* aca^2 $acab$
12/3		a^2c a^2cb	* a^2ca a^2cba	* a^2cab a^2ca^2

	1	2	3
123	* ca^2c	* ca^2ca	* ca^2ca^2

Example 2.4 Monoid containing a non-trivial non-regular $\mathscr{H}$-class

	1	2	3	4	5
a	2	1	4	3	5
b	3	4	5	5	5
ab	4	3	5	5	5
* b^2	5	5	5	5	5

Relations $a^2 = 1$ $ab = ba$ $b^2 = 0$

$$12345$$
1/2/3/4/5 $\boxed{\ast\ \ 1, a}$ $\mathbb{Z}_2$

$$345$$
1/2/345 $\boxed{b, ab}$ non-regular $\mathscr{H}$-class

$$5$$
12345 $\boxed{\ast\ 0}$

Example 2.5

	1	2	3	4	5
a	2	3	4	5	5
b	3	1	4	5	5
c	2	1	4	3	5
a^2	3	4	5	5	5
ab	1	4	5	5	5
ac	1	4	3	5	5
ba	4	2	5	5	5
b^2	4	3	5	5	5
bc	4	2	3	5	5
ca	3	2	5	4	5
cb	1	3	5	4	5
$1 = c^2$	1	2	3	4	5
a^3	4	5	5	5	5
$a^3 = a^2b$	4	5	5	5	5
$b^2 = a^2c$	4	3	5	5	5
aba	2	5	5	5	5
ab^2	3	5	5	5	5
abc	2	3	5	5	5
aca	2	5	4	5	5

	1	2	3	4	5
acb	3	5	4	5	5
ba^2	5	3	5	5	5
bab	5	1	5	5	5
bac	3	1	5	5	5
b^2a	5	4	5	5	5
$b^2a = b^3$	5	4	5	5	5
bca	5	3	4	5	5
bcb	5	1	4	5	5
$b^2 = ca^2$	4	3	5	5	5
cab	4	1	5	5	5
cac	4	1	5	3	5
cba	2	4	5	5	5
$a^2 = cb^2$	3	4	5	5	5
cbc	2	4	5	3	5
* $0 = a^4$	5	5	5	5	5
$abab$	1	5	5	5	5
* $acac$	1	5	3	5	5
$acbc$	4	5	3	5	5

	1	2	3	4	5
* baba	5	2	5	5	5
bcac	5	4	3	5	5
$ba^2 = bcb^2$	5	3	5	5	5
* bcbc	5	2	3	5	5
cabc	3	2	5	5	5
* caca	5	2	5	4	5
cacb	5	3	5	4	5
cbac	1	3	5	5	5
cbca	3	5	5	4	5
* cbcb	1	5	5	4 .	5
acbca	5	5	4	5	5
cacac	5	1	5	3	5
cacbc	5	4	5	3	5
cbcac	4	5	5	3	5
cbcbc	2	5	5	3	5
* acbcac	5	5	3	5	5
* cacbca	5	5	5	4	5
cacbcac	5	5	5	3	5

Relations

$c^2 = 1$
$a^2b = a^3$
$a^2c = b^2$
$b^3 = b^2a$
$ca^2 = b^2$
$cb^2 = a^2$
$a^4 = 0$
$aba^2 = ab^2$
$abac = abab$
$ab^2a = a^3$
$ab^2c = a^3$
$abca = a^2$
$abcb = ab$
$acab = abab$

$acba = a^3$
$ba^3 = b^2a$
$bab^2 = ba^2$
$babc = baba$
$baca = ba$
$bacb = b^2$
$b^2a^2 = 0$
$b^2ab = 0$
$b^2ac = ba^2$
$bcab = b^2a$
$bcba = baba$
$caba = baba$
$cab^2 = ba^2$
$cba^2 = ab^2$
$cbab = abab$
$ababa = aba$
$ababc = aba$
$acaca = aca$

$acacb = acb$
$acbcb = acbca$
$babab = bab$
$bcaca = acbca$
$bcacb = acbca$
$bcbca = bca$
$bcbcb = bcb$

Structure

Lattice of idempotents

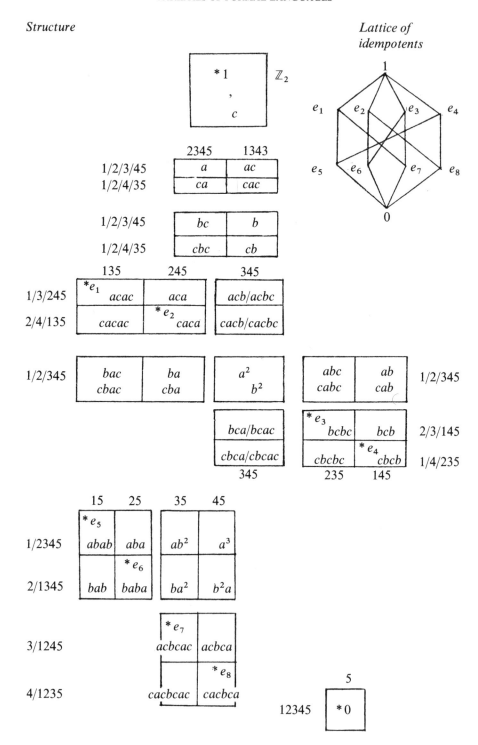

3. The Rees semigroup and the structure of regular $\mathscr{D}$-classes

Let I and J be two finite non-empty sets, G be a finite group and P be a matrix $J \times I$ with entries in G. Then $M(I, J, G, P)$, the **Rees semigroup** with G as **structure group** and P as **structure matrix**, is defined as follows: its support is $I \times G \times J$ and the law is given by the formula

$$(i, g, j)(i', g', j') = (i, gp_{ji'} g', j') \quad (\text{where} \quad P = (p_{ji})_{j \in J, i \in I})$$

More generally if P is a matrix $J \times I$ with entries in G^0, we denote by $M^0(I, J, G, P)$ the semigroup (which is still called a Rees semigroup) whose support is $I \times G \times J \cup \{0\}$ and whose law is given by the formulae

$$(i, g, j)(i', g', j') = (i, gp_{ji'} g', j') \quad \text{if} \quad p_{ji'} \neq 0$$
$$= 0 \qquad\qquad \text{if} \quad p_{ji'} = 0$$

It is easy to verify that $M^0(I, J, G, P)$ is a regular semigroup (i.e. all its elements are regular) if and only if the matrix P contains at least one non-zero entry per row and per column. We say in this case that P is regular.

A semigroup S is called **simple** if its only ideals are $\varnothing$ and S. It is called **0-simple** if it possesses a zero denoted by 0, if $S^2 \neq 0$ and if $\varnothing, \{0\}$ and S are the only ideals of S. The structure of these semigroups has been elucidated by Rees and Suschkewitsch. The following is a first characterization.

Proposition 3.1

(a) S is simple if and only if $SaS = S$ for every $a \in S$.
(b) S is 0-simple if and only if $S \neq 0$ and $SaS = S$ for every $a \in S \setminus 0$.

Proof
We shall prove only (b). The proof of (a) is similar.

Let S be a 0-simple semigroup. Then S^2 is an ideal (non-zero by definition) and therefore $S^2 = S$. It follows from this that $S^n = S$ for every $n > 0$.

Let I be the ideal of the elements of S such that $SaS = 0$. This ideal is not equal to S since

$$S = S^3 = \bigcup_{a \in S} SaS$$

Therefore $I = 0$, which means that, if $a \neq 0$, $SaS \neq 0$. Since SaS is a non-zero ideal of S, we have $SaS = S$.

Conversely, if $S \neq 0$ and if $SaS = S$ for every $a \in S$, we have $S = SaS \subset S^2$ and therefore $S^2 \neq 0$. Furthermore, if I is a non-zero ideal of S, it contains an element $a \neq 0$. We then have $S = SaS \subset SIS = I$, whence $I = S$. Therefore S is 0-simple.

The following theorem is fundamental.

Theorem 3.2

A semigroup is 0-simple if and only if it is isomorphic with a regular Rees semigroup $M^0(I, J, G, P)$. A semigroup is simple if and only if it is isomorphic with a Rees semigroup $M(I, J, G, P)$.

Proof

Let $S = M^0(I, J, G, P)$ be a regular Rees semigroup and let $a = (i, g, j)$ and $a' = (i', g', j')$ be two non-zero elements of S. Since S is regular, each row and each column of P contain a non-zero element. In particular we can find r and s such that $p_{ri} \neq 0$ and $p_{js} \neq 0$. We then have

$$(i', g^{-1}p_{ri}^{-1}, r)(i, g, j)(s, p_{js}^{-1}g', j') = (i', (g^{-1}p_{ri}^{-1})p_{ri}g p_{js}(p_{js}^{-1}g'), j')$$
$$= (i', g', j')$$

and therefore $a' \in SaS$. It follows from this that $SaS = S$ for every $a \neq 0$ and S is 0-simple.

Conversely, let S be a 0-simple semigroup. Then all the non-zero elements are $\mathscr{J}$-equivalent by Proposition 3.1 and therefore $D = S \setminus 0$ is a $\mathscr{D}$-class. Since $S^n = SE(S)S = S$, $E(S)$ does not reduce to 0 — for otherwise we would have $S^n = 0$ — and therefore D contains an idempotent. The $\mathscr{D}$-class D is therefore regular. Let $R_1, \ldots, R_m$ be the $\mathscr{R}$-classes of D, $L_1, \ldots, L_n$ be its $\mathscr{L}$-classes and $H_{ij} = R_i \cap L_j$ be its $\mathscr{H}$-classes. Let us choose the numbering so that $H_{11} = R_1 \cap L_1$ contains an idempotent e. Let us select for the moment elements $r_j \in H_{1j}$ ($1 \leq j \leq n$) and $s_i \in H_{i1}$ ($1 \leq i \leq m$). Since $e \mathscr{R} r_j$ and $e \mathscr{L} s_i$ we have $er_j = r_j$ and $s_i e = s_i$. Consequently, by Green's lemma the function $g \to s_i g r_j$ from H_{11} to H_{ij} is a bijection. It follows from this that each element $s \in S \setminus 0$ admits a unique representation of the form $s = s_i g r_j$ with $1 \leq i \leq m$, $1 \leq j \leq n$ and $g \in H_{11}$. Consider the Rees semigroup $M^0(I, J, G, P)$ where $I = \{1, \ldots, m\}$, $J = \{1, \ldots, n\}$, $G = H_{11}$ and $p_{ji} = r_j s_i$ if H_{ij} contains an idempotent and is zero otherwise. Let $\varphi : S \to M^0(I, J, G, P)$ be the mapping defined by

$$s\varphi = (i, g, j) \text{ if } s = s_i g r_j$$
$$0\varphi = 0$$

It follows, with an obvious notation, that

$$(s\varphi)(s'\varphi) = (i, g, j)(i', g', j')$$
$$= (1, g p_{ji'} g', j') \text{ if } H_{i'j} \text{ contains an idempotent}$$
$$= 0 \text{ otherwise}$$

Now, by Proposition 1.6, $ss' \in D$ if and only if $H_{i'j}$ contains an idempotent, and in this case $ss' = s_i g r_j s_i' g' r_j' = s_i g p_{ji'} g' r_j'$. Therefore φ is a morphism, bijective by construction, and hence is an isomorphism. Finally $M^0(I, J, G, P)$ is regular since each row and each column of P contain a non-zero element, because each $\mathscr{R}$-class and each $\mathscr{L}$-class of D contain an idempotent.

The case of simple semigroups can be handled in a similar manner.

A simple semigroup possesses a single $\mathscr{D}$-class which is a union of groups. It can therefore be represented as in Fig. 9.

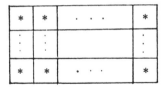

Fig. 9.

Definition 3.1
We call a **rectangular band** of size $n \times m$ the semigroup $B(n, m)$ defined on $\{1, \ldots, n\} \times \{1, \ldots, m\}$ by the law $(i, j)(i', j') = (i, j')$.

Corollary 3.3
Every simple idempotent semigroup is isomorphic to a rectangular band. In particular, in such a semigroup S we have $usv = uv$ for every $u, s, v \in S$.

Proof
It is sufficient to apply the preceding theorem, remarking that if S is idempotent the structure group of its unique regular $\mathscr{D}$-class is trivial.

One of the most important examples of a simple semigroup is given by the following proposition.

Proposition 3.4
If a regular $\mathscr{D}$-class is a semigroup, it is a simple semigroup. In particular the minimal ideal of a semigroup is a simple semigroup.

Proof
Let S be a semigroup and D a regular $\mathscr{D}$-class which is a subsemigroup of S. By Proposition 1.10 the restrictions to D of Green's relations in S and D coincide. In particular $DaD = DbD$ for every $a, b \in D$ and therefore D is simple by Proposition 3.1.

Let I be the minimal ideal of S and let $a \in I$. Then $SaS \subset SIS = I$. Since I is minimal, $SaS = I$ for every $a \in S$; therefore S is simple by Proposition 3.1.

We can generalize this last result in the following way. Let D be a regular $\mathscr{D}$-class of a semigroup S. We define a semigroup D^0 whose support is $D \cup \{0\}$ and whose law (denoted by $*$) is given by

$$s * s' = ss' \qquad \text{if } ss' \in D$$
$$= 0 \qquad \text{if } ss' \notin D$$

We then have the following proposition.

Proposition 3.5
If D is a regular $\mathscr{D}$-class of a semigroup S, D^0 is a regular 0-simple semigroup.

Proof
The proof is similar to that of Proposition 3.4.

The proposition which follows is very useful in the study of certain varieties of semigroup.

Proposition 3.6
Let $\varphi : S_1 \to S_2$ be a surjective morphism.

(a) If D_2 is a regular $\mathscr{D}$-class of S_2, there exists a regular $\mathscr{D}$-class D_1 of S such that φ induces a surjective morphism from $D_1{}^0$ onto $D_2{}^0$.
(b) If G_2 is a group in S_2, there exists a group G_1 in S_1 such that $G_1\varphi = G_2$.

Proof
(a) Let s be a minimal element (for the relation $\leq_{\mathscr{J}}$) in $D_2\varphi^{-1}$. Then $(S_1{}^1 s S_1{}^1)\varphi$ is an ideal of S_2 which intersects, and therefore contains, D_2 (for an ideal is saturated for the relation $\mathscr{J}$). Now if $t <_{\mathscr{J}} s$, $t \notin D_2\varphi^{-1}$ from the minimality of s. Hence it follows that $D_2 \subset D_1\varphi$ where D_1 is the $\mathscr{D}$-class of s. Now if $s \mathscr{D} t$, we have $s\varphi \mathscr{D} t\varphi$ and therefore $D_1\varphi \subset D_2$ and finally $D_1\varphi = D_2$. Then we can verify without difficult that φ induces a surjective morphism from $D_1{}^0$ onto $D_2{}^0$.
(b) Let S be a semigroup of minimal cardinal such that $S\varphi = G_2$ — such a semigroup exists for $G_2\varphi^{-1}\varphi = G_2$. Let $s \in S$. Then $(Ss)\varphi = G_2(s\varphi) = G_2$ and therefore $Ss = S$ from the minimality of S. Likewise $sS = S$ which shows that all the elements of S are in the same $\mathscr{H}$-class. Therefore S is a group.

We shall end this section with two useful statements.

Proposition 3.7
Let a and b be two elements of one and the same $\mathscr{H}$-class H. Then there exists a group G in S^1 and an element $g \in G$ such that $ag = b$ and $bg^{-1} = a$.

Proof
Put $M = \{s \in S^1 \mid Hs = H\}$; it is clear that M is a monoid. Let e be an idempotent of the minimal ideal of M and let G be the maximal group having e as an identity. If $h \in H$, there exists $h' \in H$ such that $h'e = h$ (since $He = H$). Hence we can deduce that $he = h'ee = h'e = h$. In other words right multiplication by e induces the identity on H.

Since $a \mathscr{H} b$ there exists $s \in S^1$ such that $as = b$. Put $ese = g$. It follows that $ag = a(ese) = ase = be = b$. Now $g \leq_{\mathscr{H}} e$ and, from the minimality of e, $g \mathscr{H} e$ and $g \in G$. Let g^{-1} be the inverse of g in G. Then we have $gg^{-1} = e$, whence $bg^{-1} = agg^{-1} = ae = a$.

Proposition 3.8

If a $\mathscr{D}$-class D, maximal for the pre-order $\leq_{\mathscr{J}}$, is not regular, it contains one element only.

Proof

Let $a, b \in D$ be such that $a \mathscr{R} b$. Then there exist $s, t \in S^1$ such that $as = b$ and $bt = a$, whence $a(st) = a$ and $a(st)^k = a$ for every $k > 0$. Let us choose k such that $e = (st)^k$ is idempotent. It follows that $ae = a$, whence $a \leq_{\mathscr{J}} e$. Since D is not regular we necessarily have $a <_{\mathscr{J}} e$ and therefore $e = 1$ and $S^1 \neq S$ from the maximality of a. From this it follows that $s = t = 1$, whence $a = b$. We could show likewise that, if $a \mathscr{L} b$, then $a = b$.

4. Varieties defined by Green's relations

Let S be a semigroup and $\mathscr{K}$ one of Green's relations. We say that S is $\mathscr{K}$-trivial if and only if $a \mathscr{K} b$ implies $a = b$.

Proposition 4.1

Let $\mathscr{K}$ be one of the Green relations $\mathscr{R}, \mathscr{L}, \mathscr{D}$ or $\mathscr{H}$ and let S be a semigroup. If the restriction of $\mathscr{K}$ to the regular $\mathscr{K}$-classes of S is trivial, then S is $\mathscr{K}$-trivial.

Proof

(a) $\mathscr{K} = \mathscr{R}$. Suppose $a \mathscr{R} b$. Then there exist $c, d \in S^1$ such that $ac = b$, $bd = a$ and whence $acd = a$. Let n be an integer such that $(cd)^n$ is idempotent. We then have $(cd)^n \mathscr{R} (cd)^n c$, whence $(cd)^n = (cd)^n c$ since the restriction of $\mathscr{R}$ to the regular $\mathscr{R}$-classes is trivial. Hence we can deduce $a = a(cd)^n = a(cd)^n c = ac = b$ and therefore S is $\mathscr{R}$-trivial.

(b) $\mathscr{K} = \mathscr{L}$. The same reasoning applies.

(c) $\mathscr{K} = \mathscr{D}$. Suppose $a \mathscr{D} b$. Then there exists $c \in S$ such that $a \mathscr{R} c$ and $c \mathscr{L} b$. Since the restriction of $\mathscr{D}$ to the regular $\mathscr{D}$-classes is trivial, restriction of $\mathscr{R}$ or $\mathscr{L}$ to the regular $\mathscr{R}$-classes or $\mathscr{L}$-classes respectively is trivial. From (a) and (b) it follows that $a = c$ and $c = b$, whence finally $a = b$. Therefore S is $\mathscr{D}$-trivial.

(d) $\mathscr{K} = \mathscr{H}$. Suppose $x \mathscr{H} y$. Then there exist $a, b, c, d \in S^1$ such that $ax = y$, $by = x$, $xc = y$, $yd = x$, whence $x = axd$ and therefore $a^n x d^n = x$ for every n. Let us choose n such that $a^n = a^{n+1}$ (which is possible since the restriction of $\mathscr{H}$ to the regular $\mathscr{H}$-classes is trivial). It follows from this that $a(a^n x d^n) = ax = a^{n+1} x d^n = a^n x d^n = x$, whence $ax = y = x$. Therefore S is $\mathscr{H}$-trivial.

We say that a semigroup S is **aperiodic** if, for every $x \in S$, there exists an integer n such that $x^n = x^{n+1}$. The proposition which follows gives various characterizations of aperiodic semigroups.

Proposition 4.2

Let S be a finite semigroup. The following conditions are equivalent.

(1) S is aperiodic (i.e. for every $x \in S$ there exists n such that $x^n = x^{n+1}$).
(2) There exists $m > 0$ such that, for every $x \in S$, $x^m = x^{m+1}$.
(3) S is $\mathscr{H}$-trivial.
(4) The groups in S are trivial.

Proof
(1) implies (2)   For each $x \in S$, let us denote by n_x the smallest integer such that $x^{n_x} = x^{n_x+1}$ and let

$$m = \max_{x \in S} n_x$$

Then $x^m = x^{m+1}$ for every $x \in S$.

(2) implies (4)   Let G be a group in S. If $x \in G$, there exists $k > 0$ such that $x(x^k) = x$. Hence we can deduce that $x = x(x^{km}) = x(x^{km+1}) = x^2 x^{km} = x^2$. Therefore x is idempotent and G is trivial.

(4) implies (3)   By Proposition 4.1, it is sufficient to verify that the restriction of $\mathscr{H}$ to the regular $\mathscr{H}$-classes is trivial. Now let H be a regular $\mathscr{H}$-class; by Green's lemma it is in bijection with a group in S. Therefore H is trivial and S is $\mathscr{H}$-trivial.

(3) implies (1)   Let $x \in S$ and T be the subsemigroup generated by x. By Chapter 1, Proposition 1.4, $T = \{x, x^2, \ldots, x^n, \ldots, x^{n+p-1}\}$ with $x^n = x^{n+p}$ and $G = \{x^n, \ldots, x^{n+p-1}\}$ is a group in T. In particular all the elements of G are $\mathscr{H}$-equivalent in T and therefore *a fortiori* in S. Since S is $\mathscr{H}$-trivial, G is trivial and $p = 1$.

We denote by A the variety of aperiodic monoids. The preceding proposition shows that we are actually concerned with a variety which is ultimately defined by the equations $x^n = x^{n+1}$.

Corollary 4.3
The variety A is ultimately defined by the equations $x^n = x^{n+1}$ $(n > 0)$.

In the same way we denote by R, R^r and J respectively the varieties of monoids which are $\mathscr{R}$-, $\mathscr{L}$- and $\mathscr{J}$-trivial. The proposition which follows gives the equations of these varieties (and shows in passing that we are actually concerned with varieties).

Proposition 4.4

(1) The variety R is ultimately defined by the equations

$$(xy)^n x = (xy)^n$$

(2) The variety R^r is ultimately defined by the equations

$$y(xy)^n = (xy)^n$$

(3) The variety $\boldsymbol{J}$ is ultimately defined by the equations

$$(xy)^n x = (xy)^n = y(xy)^n$$

It is also ultimately defined by the equations

$$(xy)^n = (yx)^n \qquad \text{and} \qquad x^n = x^{n+1}$$

Proof

(1) Let M be an $\mathcal{R}$-trivial (and therefore aperiodic) monoid and let n be such that $u^n = u^{n+1}$ for every $u \in M$. Then, for every $x, y \in M$, we have $(xy)^n x \, \mathcal{R} \, (xy)^n$ since $((xy)^n x)y = (xy)^{n+1} = (xy)^n$. Since M is $\mathcal{R}$-trivial, it follows that $(xy)^n x = (xy)^n$. Conversely, let M be a monoid satisfying the preceding equation. Let $e \in E(M)$ and $x \in M$ be such that $e \, \mathcal{R} \, x$. Then $ex = x$ and there exists y such that $xy = e$. Therefore $x = ex = (xy)^n x = (xy)^n = e$ which shows that M is $\mathcal{R}$-trivial by Propositions 4.1 and 1.9.

(2) The proof is similar.

(3) Since $\boldsymbol{J} = \boldsymbol{R} \cap \boldsymbol{R}^r$, it follows from (1) and (2) that $\boldsymbol{J}$ is ultimately defined by the equations

$$(xy)^n x = (xy)^n = y(xy)^n \tag{1}$$

Taking $y = 1$ in Eqns (1), we obtain $x^n = x^{n+1}$ and also $(xy)^n = y(xy)^n = (yx)^n y = (yx)^n$.

Conversely, suppose that a variety satisfies the equations $x^n = x^{n+1}$ and $(xy)^n = (yx)^n$. Then we have $(xy)^n = (xy)^{n+1} = (yx)^{n+1} = y(xy)^n x$, whence $(xy)^n = y^n (xy)^n x^n = y^{n+1}(xy)^n x^n = y(xy)^n$ and likewise $(xy)^n = (xy)^n x$.

The varieties of languages corresponding to these varieties of monoids will be studied in Chapter 4.

5. Relational morphisms and V-morphisms

We borrow from Tilson the following definition.

Definition 5.1

A **relational morphism** between two semigroups S and T is a relation $\tau : S \to T$ which satisfies

(i) $s\tau \neq \varnothing$ for every $s \in S$
(ii) $(s_1 \tau)(s_2 \tau) \subset (s_1 s_2)\tau$

A relational morphism τ is called **injective** ('elementary' by Tilson) if the condition $s_1 \tau \cap s_2 \tau \neq \varnothing$ implies $s_1 = s_2$ (or, equivalently, if the relation τ^{-1} is a partial function). It is called **surjective** if, for every $t \in T$, there exists $s \in S$ such that $t \in s\tau$ (i.e. if $t\tau^{-1} \neq \varnothing$). We shall constantly use the following result, which is easy to verify. If τ is a relational morphism from S into T, then its graph $R \subset S \times T$ is a subsemigroup of $S \times T$ and the projections $S \times T \to S$ and $S \times T \to T$ induce morphisms $\alpha : R \to S$ and $\beta : R \to T$ such that

(i) α is a surjective morphism
(ii) $\tau = \alpha^{-1}\beta$

The factorization $S \xrightarrow{\alpha^{-1}} R \xrightarrow{\beta} T$ is called the **canonical factorization** of τ. We can then state the following.

Proposition 5.1
Let $\tau : S \to T$ be a relational morphism and $\tau = \alpha^{-1}\beta$ its canonical factorization. Then τ is injective if and only if β is injective.

Proof
Suppose that β is injective and let $s_1, s_2 \in S$ be such that $s_1\tau \cap s_2\tau \neq \emptyset$. Then $s_1\alpha^{-1}\beta \cap s_2\alpha^{-1}\beta \neq \emptyset$, whence $s_1\alpha^{-1} \cap s_2\alpha^{-1} \neq \emptyset$ since β is injective. Since α is a function, it follows that $s_1 = s_2$.

Conversely, suppose that τ is injective and let $r_1, r_2 \in R$ be such that $r_1\beta = r_2\beta$. Since $r_1 \in r_1\alpha\alpha^{-1}$ and $r_2 \in r_2\alpha\alpha^{-1}$ it follows that $r_1\alpha\tau \cap r_2\alpha\tau \neq \emptyset$, whence $r_1\alpha = r_2\alpha$ since τ is injective, but $r_1 = (r_1\alpha, r_1\beta)$ is therefore equal to $r_2 = (r_2\alpha, r_2\beta)$.

As examples of injective relational morphisms, we can cite injective morphisms and the inverses of surjective morphisms. We have in addition the following result which justifies the terminology 'relational morphism'.

Proposition 5.2
If $\tau_1 : R \to S$ and $\tau_2 : S \to T$ are two relational morphisms then $\tau_1\tau_2 : R \to T$ is a relational morphism. If in addition τ_1 and τ_2 are injective, $\tau_1\tau_2$ is also injective.

Proof
The first assertion follows immediately from the definition. Suppose that τ_1 and τ_2 are injective. If $r_1\tau_1\tau_2 \cap r_2\tau_1\tau_2 \neq \emptyset$, there exist $s_1 \in r_1\tau_1$ and $s_2 \in r_2\tau_1$ such that $s_1\tau_2 \cap s_2\tau_2 \neq \emptyset$. From the injectivity of τ_2 we have $s_1 = s_2$ and therefore $r_1\tau_1 \cap r_2\tau_1 \neq \emptyset$, whence $r_1 = r_2$ from the injectivity of τ_1.

Corollary 5.3
Given two semigroups S and T, S divides T if and only if there exists an injective relational morphism from S into T.

Proof
If S divides T there exist morphisms $\alpha : R \to S$ and $\beta : R \to T$ with α surjective and β injective. By Proposition 1.2 $\tau = \alpha^{-1}\beta$ is an injective relational morphism from S into T.

Conversely, if τ is an injective relational morphism from S into T and if $\tau = \alpha^{-1}\beta$ is the canonical factorization of τ, Proposition 1.1 shows that β is injective. Since α is surjective, S divides T.

We return to general relational morphisms. We then have the following result.

Proposition 5.4

Let $\tau: S \to T$ be a relational morphism. If S' is a subsemigroup of S, then $S'\tau$ is a subsemigroup of T. If T' is a subsemigroup of T, then $T'\tau^{-1}$ is a subsemigroup of S.

Proof

Let $t_1, t_2 \in S'\tau$. Then there exist $s_1, s_2 \in S'$ such that $t_1 \in s_1\tau$ and $t_2 \in s_2\tau$. From this it follows that $t_1 t_2 \in (s_1\tau)(s_2\tau) \subset (s_1 s_2)\tau \subset S'\tau$ and therefore $S'\tau$ is a semigroup.

Let $s_1, s_2 \in T'\tau^{-1}$. Then there exist $t_1, t_2 \in T'$ such that $t_1 \in s_1\tau$ and $t_2 \in s_2\tau$. From this it follows as above that $t_1 t_2 \in (s_1 s_2)\tau$, whence $s_1 s_2 \in (t_1 t_2)\tau^{-1} \subset T'\tau^{-1}$ and $T'\tau^{-1}$ is a semigroup.

Let V be a variety of semigroups. We say that a (relational) morphism $\tau: S \to T$ is a (relational) V-morphism if, for every semigroup T' of T which is an element of V, $T'\tau^{-1}$ is also an element of V. Then we have the following proposition.

Proposition 5.5

Let V be a variety of semigroups, $\tau: S \to T$ be a relational morphism and $\tau = \alpha^{-1}\beta$ be its canonical factorization. Then τ is a relational V-morphism if and only if β is a V-morphism.

Proof

Let T' be a subsemigroup of T, an element of V. If β is a V-morphism, then $T'\beta^{-1} \in V$ and therefore $T'\beta^{-1}\alpha = T'\tau^{-1} \in V$ since α is surjective. Conversely, suppose that τ is a relational V-morphism and let $\tau \times 1_T: S \times T \to T \times T$ be defined by $(s,t)(\tau \times 1_T) = s\tau \times t$. Put $T'' = \{(t,t) \mid t \in T'\}$. It follows that

$$T''(\tau \times 1_T)^{-1} = \{(s,t) \in S \times T \mid t \in s\tau \text{ and } t \in T'\}$$
$$= R' \subset T'\tau^{-1} \times T'$$

Since $T'\tau^{-1} \times T' \in V$, we also have $R' \in V$. Now we have, by definition of R and β,

$$T'\beta^{-1} = \{(s,t) \in S \times T \mid t \in s\tau \text{ and } t \in T'\} = R'$$

Therefore β is a V-morphism.

Proposition 5.6

If $\tau_1: R \to S$ and $\tau_2: S \to T$ are relational V-morphisms, then $\tau_1\tau_2: R \to T$ is a relational V-morphism.

Proof

This is immediate.

By Proposition 5.5, an injective relational morphism is a relational **V**-morphism for every variety **V** of semigroups. (This is the case in particular for the inverse of a surjective morphism.) The converse is false, as the following example shows.

Let $N_3 = \{0, x, y\}$ and $N_2 = \{0, a\}$ be the commutative nilpotent semigroups with three and two elements respectively. Let $\varphi: N_3 \to N_2$ be defined by $x\varphi = y\varphi = a$, $0\varphi = 0$. φ is a surjective morphism and, for every variety V, φ is a V-morphism; in fact we have on the one hand $0\varphi^{-1} = 0$ and on the other hand $N_2\varphi^{-1} = N_3 < N_2 \times N_2$.

However, φ is not injective.

If **V** is the variety **A** of aperiodic semigroups, a **V**-morphism is called an **aperiodic (relational) morphism**.

The last part of this section presents a certain number of statements concerning relational **V**-morphisms. In all these statements, $\tau: S \to T$ denotes a relational morphism and $\tau = \alpha^{-1}\beta$ (with $\alpha: R \to S$ and $\beta: R \to T$) is its canonical factorization.

Proposition 5.7

The following conditions are equivalent.

(i) τ is aperiodic.
(ii)   For every idempotent $e \in T$, $e\tau^{-1}$ is aperiodic.
(iii)   The restriction of τ to each group in S is injective.
(iv)   The restriction of τ to each regular $\mathscr{H}$-class of S is injective.

Moreover, we obtain four equivalent conditions (i)′–(iv)′ by replacing τ by β and S by R in (i)–(iv).

Before tackling the proof we recall that by a regular $\mathscr{H}$-class we mean an $\mathscr{H}$-class contained in a regular $\mathscr{D}$-class.

Proof

The equivalence of (i) and (i)′ results from Proposition 5.5 and the implications (i) $\Rightarrow$ (ii) and (iv) $\Rightarrow$ (iii) are obvious.

(iii) implies (i)   Let T' be an aperiodic semigroup of T. Put $S' = T'\tau^{-1}$ and let H be a group in S'. Then there exists a group H' in R such that $H'\alpha = H$. $H'\beta$ is therefore a group in T'; since T' is aperiodic $H'\beta$ is reduced to a single element $\{e\}$. Let $h_1, h_2 \in H$ and $h_1', h_2' \in H'$ be such that $h_1'\alpha = h_1$ and $h_2'\alpha = h_2$. We have $e = h_1'\beta = h_2'\beta \in h_1\tau \cap h_2\tau$. Since the restriction of τ to the groups of S is injective, we can deduce from this that $h_1 = h_2$ which shows that H is trivial. Therefore S' is aperiodic.

(ii) implies (iv)   Given a regular $\mathscr{H}$-class H, there exists an element $a \in S$ such that the function $h \to ha$ is a bijection from H onto a group G with e as an identity. Let $h_1, h_2 \in H$ be two elements such that $h_1\tau \cap h_2\tau \neq \varnothing$. Then we have

$$\varnothing = (h_1\tau \cap h_2\tau)(a\tau) \subset (h_1\tau)(a\tau) \cap (h_2\tau)(a\tau) \subset (h_1 a)\tau \cap (h_2 a)\tau$$

If we put $g_1 = h_1 a$, $g_2 = h_2 a$ and $g = g_2 g_1{}^{-1}$ we obtain in the same way $\varnothing \neq (g_1\tau \cap g_2\tau)(g_1{}^{-1}\tau) \subset e\tau \cap g\tau$. Furthermore, we have

$$(e\tau \cap g\tau)(e\tau \cap g\tau) \subset (e\tau \cap g\tau)e\tau \subset (e\tau)(e\tau) \cap (g\tau)(e\tau) \subset (ee)\tau \cap (ge)\tau = e\tau \cap g\tau$$

which proves that $e\tau \cap g\tau$ is a non-empty semigroup. If f is an idempotent of $e\tau \cap g\tau$, we have $e, g \in f\tau^{-1}$, whence $e = g$ since $f\tau^{-1}$ is aperiodic. Hence we can deduce that $g_1 = g_2$ and then $h_1 = h_2$ which proves (iv).

The equivalence of the statements (i)–(iv) results from this. Applying this first theorem to β, we can deduce from this the equivalence of the conditions (i)′–(iv)′ which completes the proof.

The proposition which follows gives various characterizations of relational V-morphisms when V is the variety LG of semigroups which are locally groups.

Proposition 5.8
The following conditions are equivalent.

(i) τ is a relational LG-morphism.
(ii)   For every idempotent $e \in T$, $e\tau^{-1} \in LG$.
(iii) β is an LG-morphism.
(iv)   For every idempotent $e \in T$, $e\beta^{-1} \in LG$.
(v)   For all *regular* elements a, b of R, the condition $a\beta \mathscr{D} b\beta$ (in $R\beta$) implies $a \mathscr{D} b$.

We recall that a semigroup S is locally a group if and only if all the idempotents of S are contained within the minimal ideal of S, or, equivalently, if all the idempotents of S are $\mathscr{J}$-equivalent.

Proof
The implication (i) $\Rightarrow$ (ii) is obvious.
(ii) implies (i)   Let T' be a subsemigroup of T, an element of LG. Then $T' \cap S\tau$ is again an element of LG. In other words, we can go back to the case in which $T' \subset S\tau$. Let $\bar{\tau}: T'\tau^{-1} \to T'$ be the relational morphism defined by $s\bar{\tau} = s\tau \cap T'$ (see Problem 5.4) and let $e, f \in T'\tau^{-1}$ be two idempotents. Since $e\bar{\tau}$ and $f\bar{\tau}$ are non-empty semigroups, there exist idempotents $e', f' \in T'$ such that $e' \in e\bar{\tau}$ and $f' \in f\bar{\tau}$. Now, since $T' \in LG$ we have $e' \mathscr{J} f'$. In particular there exist elements $a', b' \in T'$ such that $e' = a' f' b'$. Let $a, b \in T'\tau^{-1}$ be such that $a' \in a\tau$ and $b' \in b\tau$. It follows from this that $e' = a'f'b' \in (a\tau)(f\tau)(b\tau) \subset (afb)\tau$ and therefore $e, afb \in e'\tau^{-1}$. However, by (ii) $e'\tau^{-1} \in LG$ and consequently the idempotent e is in the minimal ideal of $e'\tau^{-1}$. It follows from this that $e \leq_{\mathscr{J}} afb \leq_{\mathscr{J}} f$ in $T'\tau^{-1}$. We could show in the same way that $f \leq_{\mathscr{J}} e$ and therefore finally $e \mathscr{J} f$ which proves that $T'\tau^{-1} \in LG$.

We have therefore established the equivalence (i) $\Leftrightarrow$ (ii). Taking $\tau = \beta$ we obtain the equivalence (iii) $\Leftrightarrow$ (iv) and Proposition 5.5 ensures that (i) is equivalent to (iii).

It is now necessary to study condition (v).

(iv) implies (v) Let a and b be two regular elements such that $a\beta \mathscr{D} b\beta$ and let e and f respectively be idempotents of the $\mathscr{D}$-class of a and b. We have also $e\beta \mathscr{D} f\beta$. In particular there exist elements $c\beta$ and $d\beta$ such that $e\beta = (cfd)\beta$. It follows from this that $e, cfd \in e\beta^{-1}$ and as $e\beta^{-1} \in \boldsymbol{LG}$ by (iv) we have $e \leq_{\mathscr{J}} cfd \leq_{\mathscr{J}} f$. Similar reasoning leads to the conclusion that $f \leq_{\mathscr{J}} e$ and therefore $e \mathscr{D} f$ and finally $a \mathscr{D} b$.

(v) implies (iv) Let e be an idempotent of T and let e_1, e_2 be two idempotents of $e\beta^{-1}$. Since $e_1\beta = e_2\beta = e$ we have *a fortiori* $e_1\beta \mathscr{D} e_2\beta$. From (v) it follows that $e_1 \mathscr{D} e_2$ which shows that $e\beta^{-1} \in \boldsymbol{LG}$.

Corollary 5.9
Let $\varphi:S \to T$ be a surjective $\boldsymbol{LG}$-morphism. Then S and T have the same number of regular $\mathscr{D}$-classes.

Proof
Let $d(S)$ and $d(T)$ be the numbers of regular $\mathscr{D}$-classes of S and T respectively. Since the image under φ of a regular $\mathscr{D}$-class is a regular $\mathscr{D}$-class we have $d(T) \leq d(S)$. Furthermore, condition (v) of Proposition 5.8 states that $a\varphi \mathscr{D} b\varphi$ implies $a \mathscr{D} b$. Consequently $d(S) \leq d(T)$.

A (relational) $\boldsymbol{LI}$-morphism is called a locally trivial (relational) morphism.

Corollary 5.10
Let $\tau:S \to T$ be a relational morphism. The following conditions are equivalent.

(1) τ is locally trivial
(2) For every $e \in E(T)$, $e\tau^{-1}$ is locally trivial.

Proof
This follows immediately from Propositions 5.7 and 5.8, since $\boldsymbol{LI} = \boldsymbol{LG} \cap \boldsymbol{A}$.

We have analogous results for the varieties $\boldsymbol{K}$, $\boldsymbol{K^r}$ and $\boldsymbol{Nil}$.

Proposition 5.11
Let $\tau:S \to T$ be a relational morphism and let $\boldsymbol{V}$ be one of the varieties $\boldsymbol{K}$, $\boldsymbol{K^r}$ and $\boldsymbol{Nil}$. Then τ is a relational $\boldsymbol{V}$-morphism if and only if $e\tau^{-1} \in \boldsymbol{V}$ for every $e \in E(T)$.

Proof
First take $\boldsymbol{V} = \boldsymbol{K}$. The condition is obviously necessary. Conversely suppose that $e\tau^{-1} \in \boldsymbol{K}$ for every $e \in E(T)$. Then since $\boldsymbol{K} \subset \boldsymbol{LI}$, τ is locally trivial by Corollary 5.10. Let $T' \in \boldsymbol{K}$ be a subsemigroup of T and put $S' = T'\tau^{-1}$. Let e and f be two $\mathscr{R}$-equivalent idempotents of S'. Since $S' = (T'\beta^{-1})\alpha$, we can find, by Pro-

position 3.6, two idempotents $\bar{e}, \bar{f}$ of $T\beta^{-1}$ such that $\bar{e}\,\mathscr{R}\,\bar{f}$, $\bar{e}\alpha = e$ and $\bar{f}\alpha = f$. Consequently, $\bar{e}\beta$ and $\bar{f}\beta$ are two $\mathscr{R}$-equivalent idempotents of T' and, since $T' \in K$, $\bar{e}\beta = \bar{f}\beta = e' \in E(T')$. We can deduce from this that $e, f \in e'\tau^{-1}$ and therefore $e = f$ since $e'\tau^{-1} \in K$. Therefore S' is a locally trivial semigroup (for τ is locally trivial) and $\mathscr{R}$-trivial. Therefore $S' \in K$, which completes the proof.

For $V = K^r$ the proof is similar. Finally the case $V = Nil$ is obtained by noting that $Nil = K \cap K^r$.

It must not be thought, in view of the preceding results, that all the varieties V have the property '$\tau : S \to T$ is a relational V-morphism if and only if $e\tau^{-1} \in V$ for all $e \in E(T)$'. In fact there follow some counter-examples.

Example 5.1
Let $S = N_2 = \{0, a\}$ be the nilpotent semigroup with two elements, let $T = \mathbb{Z}_2 = \{1, -1\}$ and let τ be the relational morphism from S into T defined by $a\tau = \{-1\}$ and $0\tau = \{1, -1\}$. Since $1\tau^{-1} = 0$, we have $1\tau^{-1} \in G$. However, τ is not a relational G-morphism since $T\tau^{-1} = S \notin G$.

Example 5.2 (S. Margolis)
Let S be the semigroup generated by the following transformations a and b:

	1	2	3	4	5	6	0
a	2	5	4	0	5	2	0
b	5	1	0	3	5	3	0

The $\mathscr{D}$-classes structure of this semigroup is the following:

	2450	1350
16/25/40/3	* a	ab
15/46/30/2	ba	* b

	50
1256/340	* a^2
125/3460	* b^2

Let $T = \{a^2, b^2\}$ be the minimal ideal of S and let $\varphi : S \to T$ be the morphism defined by $a\varphi = a^2$, $b\varphi = b^2$. Then we have $a^2\varphi^{-1} = \{a^2, a, ab\}$ and $b^2\varphi^{-1} = \{b^2, b, ba\}$, and therefore, for every idempotent $e \in T$, $e\varphi^{-1} \in J \subset R$. However, φ is not an R-morphism, for $T \in R$ and $T\varphi^{-1} = S \notin R$. The relational morphisms enable us to introduce a new operation on varieties, denoted by $V^{-1}W$, whose definition depends on the following result.

Proposition 5.12

Let V be a variety of semigroups and W a variety of semigroups (or monoids). Then the class S of semigroups (or monoids) such that there exists a relational V-morphism $\tau : S \to T$ with $T \in W$ is a variety of semigroups (or monoids) which we denote by $V^{-1}W$.

Proof

Let $S \in V^{-1}W$. Then there exists a relational V-morphism $\tau : S \to T$ with $T \in W$. If $\varphi : R \to S$ is an injective morphism, φ is a relational V-morphism and therefore $\varphi \tau : R \to T$ is a relational V-morphism. Consequently $R \in V^{-1}W$. If $\beta : S \to R'$ is a surjective morphism, β^{-1} is an injective relational morphism and therefore a relational V-morphism. Consequently $\beta^{-1}\tau : R' \to T$ is a V-morphism and $R' \in V^{-1}W$. Finally, let $S_1, S_2 \in V^{-1}W$. There exist two relational V-morphisms $\tau_1 : S_1 \to T_1$, $\tau_2 : S_2 \to T_2$ with $T_1, T_2 \in W$. Then $\tau_1 \times \tau_2 : S_1 \times S_2 \to T_1 \times T_2$ is a relational V-morphism and $S_1 \times S_2 \in V^{-1}W$.

We shall now give some examples of varieties of the form $V^{-1}W$. First, we need a property. If S is a semigroup, we denote by $2^{E(S)}$ the semigroup of subsets of $E(S)$ together with the operation of intersection.

Proposition 5.13

(1) If S is $\mathcal{R}$-trivial, $\pi : S \to 2^{E(S)}$ defined by $s\pi = \{e \in E(S) \mid es = e\}$ is a surjective K-morphism.

(2) If S is $\mathcal{L}$-trivial, $\pi : S \to 2^{E(S)}$ defined by $s\pi = \{e \in E(S) \mid se = e\}$ is a surjective K^r-morphism.

(3) If S is $\mathcal{J}$-trivial, $\pi : S \to 2^{E(S)}$ defined by $s\pi = \}e \in E(S) \mid es = e = se\}$ is a surjective Nil-morphism.

(4) If each regular $\mathcal{D}$-class of S is an independent subsemigroup, then $\pi : S \to 2^{E(S)}$ defined by $s\pi = \}e \in E(S) \mid ese = e\}$ is a surjective LI-morphism.

Proof

(1) If $e \in (s_1 s_2)\pi$, we have $es_1 s_2 = e$, whence $e \mathcal{R} es_1$. Since S is $\mathcal{R}$-trivial, $es_1 = e = es_2$ and therefore $e \in s_1 \pi \cap s_2 \pi$. Conversely, if $e \in s_1 \pi \cap s_2 \pi$, $es_1 = e = es_2$, whence $es_1 s_2 = e$, i.e. $e \in (s_1 s_2)\pi$. Therefore π is a morphism. Fix $A \in 2^{E(S)}$ and let $x, y \in A\pi^{-1}$. Let x^ω be the idempotent of the semigroup generated by x. Then $x^\omega x = x^\omega$ since S is aperiodic and therefore $x^\omega \in x\pi = A$. Consequently $x^\omega y = x^\omega$ since $y\pi = A$. It follows from this that $A\pi^{-1}$ satisfies the equation $x^\omega y = x^\omega$, i.e. $A\pi^{-1} \in K$.

(2) The proof is similar.

(3) We can easily adapt the proof from (1) by noting that $Nil = K \cap K^r$.

(4) Let $e \in (s_1 s_2)\pi$. Then $es_1 s_2 e = e$, whence $es_1 \mathcal{R} e$ and $s_2 e \mathcal{L} e$, and therefore $es_1 e = e = es_2 e$ since the $\mathcal{D}$-class of e only contains idempotents. Conversely if $es_1 e = e = es_2 e$ we have $es_1 \mathcal{R} e \mathcal{L} s_2 e$ and, as the $\mathcal{D}$-class of e is a semigroup, we have $es_1 s_2 e \in R_{es_1} \cap L_{s_2 e} = R_e \cap L_e = H_e = \{e\}$ and therefore $es_1 s_2 e = e$. We can deduce from the above that π is a morphism. Fis $A \in 2^{E(S)}$ and let $x, y \in A\pi^{-1}$. We

obtain by the same argument as in (1) that $x^\omega y x^\omega = x^\omega$ and therefore $A\pi^{-1} \in LI$.

We denote by DA the class of semigroups of which each regular $\mathscr{D}$-class is an idempotent semigroup (or aperiodic semigroup, which is equivalent in this case).

Proposition 5.14
DA is a variety of semigroups.

Proof
Let $S \in DA$, R be a subsemigroup of S and D be a regular $\mathscr{D}$-class of R. Let $a \in D$; then $a \mathscr{R}_T e$ for some $e \in E(T)$ and therefore $a \mathscr{R}_S e$. However, the $\mathscr{D}$-class of e in S only contains idempotents and therefore $a \in E(R)$. Therefore $R \in DA$.

Let $\varphi: S \to T$ be a surjective morphism and let D be a regular $\mathscr{D}$-class of T. By Proposition 3.6 there exists a regular $\mathscr{D}$-class D' of S such that $D'\varphi = D$. Since D' only contains idempotents, D also only contains idempotents.

Finally let $S_1, S_2 \in DA$. We can easily see that the $\mathscr{D}$-classes of $S_1 \times S_2$ are of the form $D_1 \times D_2$ where D_i is a $\mathscr{D}$-class of S_i $(i = 1, 2)$. Therefore if $D_1 \subset E(S_1)$ and $D_2 \subset E(S_2)$, $D_1 \times D_2 \subset E(S_1 \times S_2)$ and therefore $S_1 \times S_2 \in DA$.

Proposition 5.15
The following equalities hold: $J = Nil^{-1}J_1$, $R = K^{-1}J_1$, $R^r = (K^r)^{-1}J_1$ and $DA = LI^{-1}J_1$.

Proof
The inclusions $J \subset Nil^{-1}J_1$, $R \subset K^{-1}J_1$, etc. follow from Proposition 5.13. The opposite inclusions can all be proved in the same way. By way of example, we give the proof that $LI^{-1}J_1 \subset DA$. If $S \in LI^{-1}J_1$, there exists a locally trivial relational morphism $\tau: S \to T$ with $T \in J_1$. If $\tau = \alpha^{-1}\beta$ is the canonical factorization of τ we know that $\beta: R \to T$ is locally trivial and that S is a quotient of R. It suffices therefore to verify that $R \in DA$. Let D be a regular $\mathscr{D}$-class of R. Then $D\beta$ is a regular $\mathscr{D}$-class of T. Since T is idempotent and commutative, $D\beta$ is reduced to an idempotent e and therefore $D \subset e\tau^{-1}$. Since $e\tau^{-1}$ is locally trivial, D only contains idempotents. Therefore $R \in DA$.

Problems

Section 1

1.1   Let S be the infinite semigroup of matrices of the form

$$\begin{pmatrix} a & 0 \\ b & 1 \end{pmatrix}$$

where $a, b \in Q$, $a > 0$, $b > 0$, together with the usual matrix multiplication. Show that, in S, $\mathscr{R} = \mathscr{L} = \mathscr{H} = \mathscr{D}$ and that these four relations coincide with equality. In contrast, $\mathscr{J}$ is the universal relation.

1.2 Let M be a finite monoid. Show that the $\mathscr{D}$-class of the identity is a group (i.e. an $\mathscr{H}$-class).

1.3 Let a be a regular element of S (finite) and let s be such that $asa = a$. Show that a and $a' = sas$ satisfy the relations $aa'a = a$ and $a'aa' = a'$ (we say that a and a' are inverses or that a' is *an* inverse of a). Show by an example that an element can have several inverses.

1.4 Let a and b be two elements of one and the same regular $\mathscr{D}$-class. Show that H_b contains an inverse of a if and only if the $\mathscr{H}$-classes $R_a \cap L_b$ and $L_a \cap R_b$ contain an idempotent. Show that, if this condition holds, H_b contains only one inverse of a. Deduce from this that the number of inverses of an element $a \in S$ is equal to the product of the number of idempotents of R_a with the number of idempotents of L_a.

1.5 A semigroup S is called **inverse** if each element of S has only one inverse. Show the equivalence of the following conditions.
  (1) S is inverse.
  (2) Each $\mathscr{R}$-class and each $\mathscr{L}$-class of S contain exactly one idempotent.
  (3) S is regular and the idempotents of S commute.

1.6 Let S be an inverse semigroup. We denote by a^{-1} the inverse of $a \in S$. Establish the following formulae:

$$(a^{-1})^{-1} = a \qquad\qquad (ab)^{-1} = b^{-1}a^{-1}$$

1.7 Show that a semigroup is inverse if and only if it is a regular subsemigroup of a semigroup $\mathscr{I}_n$ ($\mathscr{I}_n$ is the semigroup of (partial) injective functions from $\{1,\dots,n\}$ into itself). (Hint: associate with each $a \in S$ the function $\rho_a : S \to S$ defined on Sa^{-1} by $x\rho_a = xa$.)

1.8 Show that inverse semigroups *do not form* a variety. We denote by **Inv** the variety *generated* by the inverse semigroups. Show that if $S \in \textbf{Inv}$ the idempotents of S commute.

1.9 (*Ash*) Show that, if the idempotents of S commute, then $S \in \textbf{Inv}$. (Hint: read the paper 'Finite semigroups with commuting idempotents' by C. J. Ash (*J. Aust. Math. Soc., Series A*, in the press).)

1.10 Let S be a subsemigroup of T and let $a, b \in S$ with b regular in S. Then, if $a \leq_{\mathscr{R}} b$ or $a \leq_{\mathscr{L}} b$ or $a \leq_{\mathscr{H}} b$ in T, $a \leq_{\mathscr{R}} b$ or $a \leq_{\mathscr{L}} b$ or $a \leq_{\mathscr{H}} b$ respectively in S.
  Show that this result is false for the relation $\leq_{\mathscr{J}}$. (Take $T = S(ab)^*$ on $A = \{a, b\}$: T has five elements, of which three are idempotents e, f and 0 which constitute a subsemigroup of S. We have then $e \leq_{\mathscr{J}} f$ (and even $e \mathscr{J} f$) in T, but this relation is not satisfied in S.)

1.11 Let S be an *ideal* of T and let $\mathscr{K}$ be one of the relations $\mathscr{R}$, $\mathscr{L}$, $\mathscr{H}$ or $\mathscr{J}$. If $a \leq_{\mathscr{K}} b$, if $b \in S$ and if a or b is regular in T, then $a \leq_{\mathscr{K}} b$ in S.

Section 2

2.1 Consider again the syntactic semigroups calculated in Chapter 1, Problem 2.2. Calculate the regular $\mathscr{D}$-classes of these semigroups.

2.2 Take a rational language at random. Calculate its minimal automaton and then its syntactic semigroup by studying in detail the regular $\mathscr{D}$-classes.

Section 3

3.1 Show that in a simple semigroup, $ax = bx$ and $xa = xb$ implies $a = b$.

3.2 Show that the simple semigroups form a variety. Determine its equations.

Section 4

4.1 Let H be a variety of groups. We denote by $\bar{H}$ the class of monoids M such that, if G is a group in M, then $G \in H$. Show that $\bar{H}$ is a variety of monoids. (We say that it is the **group variety** defined by H. In particular if H is the trivial variety, $\bar{H} = A$.)

4.2 Let DS be the class of semigroups of which each regular $\mathscr{D}$-class is a (simple) semigroup. Show that DS is a variety defined by the equations

$$((xy)^\omega (yx)^\omega (xy)^\omega)^\omega = (xy)^\omega.$$

4.3 A 0-simple semigroup is **flat** if it is isomorphic to a Rees semigroup $M^0(I, J, G, P)$ where the non-zero entries of the matrix P are all equal to 1, the identity of G. Show that S is flat if and only if the semigroup generated by $E(S)$ is aperiodic.

4.4 (Difficult) A regular $\mathscr{D}$-class D of a semigroup is called flat if D^0 is a flat semigroup (cf. Exercise 4.3). A semigroup S is called flat if all its $\mathscr{D}$-classes are flat. Show that S is flat if and only if the semigroup generated by $E(S)$ is aperiodic (Tilson, 1973).

Section 5

5.1 We say that a submonoid L^* (not necessarily free) of A^* is pure if and only if $u^n \in L^*$ with $u \in A^*$ and $n > 0$ implies $u \in L^*$. In this case we call the operation $L \to L^*$ **pure star**.

(a) Show that if L^* is pure, there exists an aperiodic relational morphism $\tau : M(L^*) \to M(L)$.

(b) Let X be an aperiodic code (i.e. such that $M(X)$ is aperiodic). Show that X^* is pure if and only if X^* is aperiodic.

5.2 Let X be a finite code. We denote by $MP(X^*)$ or $SP(X^*)$ respectively the petal monoid or semigroup of X, i.e. the monoid or semigroup of unambiguous relations obtained starting from the petal automaton of X.

(a) Show that there exist surjective morphisms

$$\varphi: MP(X^*) \to M(X^*)$$
$$\psi: SP(X^+) \to S(X^+)$$

(b) Show that φ is an aperiodic morphism and that ψ is a locally trivial morphism ($\equiv$ **LI**-morphism).

(c) Hence deduce that $SP(X^+)$ and $S(X^+)$ have the same number of regular $\mathscr{D}$-classes and that, if D is a regular $\mathscr{D}$-class of $SP(X^*)$, the $\mathscr{D}$-classes D and $D\psi$ have the same structure group.

5.3 If S is a semigroup, we denote by $\mathscr{P}(S)$ the semigroup of subsets of S, together with the product $A \cdot B = \{ab \mid a \in A, b \in B\}$. If $\varphi: S \to T$ is a morphism, we define a morphism $\bar{\varphi}: \mathscr{P}(S) \to \mathscr{P}(T)$ by putting $A\bar{\varphi} = \{a\varphi \mid a \in A\}$. Show that if φ is locally trivial, $\bar{\varphi}$ is aperiodic.

5.4 Let $\tau: S \to T$ be a relational morphism and let τ' be a subsemigroup of T. Show that the relation $\bar{\tau}: T'\tau^{-1} \to T'$ defined by $s\bar{\tau} = s\tau \cap T'$ is a relational morphism. Show that if τ is injective, $\bar{\tau}$ is injective.

5.5 Let G and H be two finite groups and let $\tau: G \to H$ be a surjective relational morphism. Show that $G' = 1\tau^{-1}$ is a normal subgroup of G, $H' = 1\tau$ is a normal subgroup of H and $G/G' = H/H'$.

5.6 Let $\tau: S \to T$ be a relational morphism, G be a group in S and H be a group in the minimal ideal of $G\tau$. Then the relation $\sigma: G \to H$ defined by $g\sigma = g\tau \cap H$ induces a relational morphism from G onto H.

5.7 Let A_1 be the variety of idempotent monoids.

(1) Verify that A_1 is indeed a variety by determining its equations.

(2) Show that $\tau: S \to T$ is a relational A_1-morphism if and only if, for every $e \in E(T)$, $e\tau^{-1} \in A_1$.

5.8 Let $\tau: S \to T$ be a relational morphism. Show that τ is locally trivial if and only if, for every $e \in E(S)$ and $s \in S$, $(ese)\tau \cap e\tau \neq \varnothing$ implies $e = ese$.

5.9 Show that **DA** is defined by the equation $(xy)^\omega (yx)^\omega (xy)^\omega = (xy)^\omega$ or again by the equations $(xy)^\omega x(xy)^\omega = (xy)^\omega = (xy)^\omega y(xy)^\omega$.

5.10 Show that if V and W are varieties of semigroups, we have $V^{-1}(V^{-1}W) = V^{-1}W$.

5.11 Prove the following results.

(a) **Nil$^{-1}K^1$** is the variety defined by the equations $x^\omega y = x^\omega = (xy)^\omega$.

(b) **Nil$^{-1}K^r{}_1$** is the variety defined by the equations $yx^\omega = x^\omega = (yx)^\omega$.

(c) **Nil$^{-1}LI_1$** is the variety defined by the equations $x^\omega yx^\omega = x^\omega$ and $x^\omega (yx)^\omega = x^\omega = (xy)^\omega x^\omega$.

(d) **K$^{-1}K^r{}_1$** is the variety defined by the equations $x^\omega yx^\omega = x^\omega$ and $x^\omega y^\omega = x^\omega (zy)^\omega$.

(e) **K$^{-1}K^r = (K^r)^{-1}K = LI$**.

5.12 Show that $J_1{}^{-1}G = Inv$ (cf. Problem 1.8).

5.13 Let $\tau: S \to T$ be an injective relational morphism. Prove that $(E(T))\tau^{-1} = E(S)$.

Chapter 4

Piecewise-testable Languages and Star-free Languages

This chapter is dominated by two fundamental theorems in the theory of varieties of languages: the theorem of I. Simon and the theorem of Schützenberger.

Simon's theorem enables us to describe the variety of languages corresponding to the variety of monoids J. It has numerous applications in the theories of languages and of semigroups, in particular a representation theorem for $\mathcal{J}$-trivial monoids due to H. Straubing. The proof of Simon's theorem rests on a remarkable combinatorial result involving words, which itself merits a digression.

Schützenberger's theorem enables us to describe the variety of languages corresponding to the variety of monoids A. Two proofs of it are known. Schützenberger's proof, which is presented here, is achieved through induction on the cardinality of the syntactic monoid and uses the whole battery of Green's relations. The other proof, which is based on decompositions of semigroups in terms of the wreath product, was found independently by Cohen-Brzozowski and A. Meyer. It is discussed in Eilenberg's book.

Finally we have included Eilenberg's description of varieties of languages corresponding to the varieties of monoids R and R^r in this chapter (see also the article by Brzozowski and Fich on this subject).

1. Piecewise-testable languages; Simon's theorem

In this section we shall describe the variety of languages $\mathcal{J}$ associated with J. Let A be an alphabet. We recall that a word $a_1 \ldots a_k \in A^*$ is a subword of a word v of A^* if there exist words $v_0, v_1, \ldots, v_k \in A^*$ such that $v = v_0 a_1 v_1 \ldots a_k v_k$. For each integer $n \geq 0$, we define an equivalence relation $\sim_n$ on A^* by $u \sim_n v$ if and only if u and v have the same set of subwords of length less than or equal to n.

For example $abbac \sim_1 cab$ and $ababab \sim_3 bababa$.

We can easily verify that $\sim_n$ is a congruence with finite index (the number of classes is bounded by 2^N where N is the number of words of length less than or equal to n).

Definition 1.1
A language is called piecewise testable if it is the union of classes modulo $\sim_n$ for a certain integer n.

The terminology chosen can be explained thus: L is piecewise testable if there exists an integer n such that we can test whether a word belongs to L by simple inspection of its subwords of length less than or equal to n. The following is a first description of these languages.

Proposition 1.1
A language L of A^* is piecewise testable if and only if it is in the boolean algebra generated by the languages of the form $A^*q_1A^*a_2\ldots A^*a_nA^*$ where $n \geq 0$ and the a_i are letters.

Proof
Let u be a word of A^*. A moment's reflection enables us to verify the equality

$$\{v \in A^* | v \sim_n u\} = (\cap\, A^*a_1A^*a_2\ldots a_mA^*)\backslash(\cup\, A^*a_1A^*a_2\ldots a_mA^*)$$

where the intersection (union) is taken over the set of m-tuples $(a_1,\ldots,a_m)$ such that $0 \leq m \leq n$ and such that $a_1\ldots a_m$ is (is not) a subword of u. From this it follows that if L is a union of classes modulo $\sim_n$, L is in the boolean algebra generated by the languages of the form $A^*a_1A^*\ldots a_nA^*$.

Conversely let $L = A^*a_1A^*\ldots a_nA^*$ and let $u \in L$; then $a_1\ldots a_n$ is a subword of u. Therefore if $u \sim_n v$, $a_1\ldots a_n$ is a subword of v and $v \in L$. This shows that L is saturated by $\sim_n$, and therefore is a (finite) union of classes modulo $\sim_n$.

The syntactic characterization of piecewise-testable languages rests on properties of the congruence $\sim_n$ which we shall now expound.

Proposition 1.2
Let $u, v \in A^*$ and $a \in A$. Then if $uav \sim_{2n-1} uv$, $ua \sim_n u$ or $av \sim_n v$.

Proof
Suppose that $u \not\sim_n ua$ and $v \not\sim_n av$. Then there exists a word x of length less than or equal to n which is a subword of ua but not of u. Likewise there exists a word y of length n which is a subword of av but not of v. Necessarily we have $x = x'a$ and $y = ay'$ and the word $x'ay'$ of length less than or equal to $2n-1$ is a subword of uav but not of uv. Therefore $uav \not\sim_{2n-1} uv$.

If u is a word, we denote by $u\alpha$ the alphabet of u, i.e. the set of letters a such that $|u|_a > 0$.

Proposition 1.3

Let $u, v \in A^*$ and $n > 0$. Then $u \sim_n vu$ if and only if there exist $u_1, \ldots, u_n \in A^*$ such that $u = u_1 \ldots u_n$ and $v\alpha \subset u_1\alpha \subset \ldots \subset u_n\alpha$.

Proof

First of all the result is trivial if $u = 1$. We shall suppose from now on that $u \in A^+$. We shall show that the condition is *necessary* by induction on n. If $n = 1$, $u \sim_1 vu$ implies $u\alpha = (vu)\alpha$ and therefore $v\alpha \subset u\alpha$. Suppose that $u \sim_{n+1} vu$ and let u_{n+1} be the shortest right factor of u such that $u_{n+1}\alpha = u\alpha$. Since $u \in A^+$, $u\alpha$ is non-empty and therefore $u_{n+1} \in A^+$. Put $u_{n+1} = au'$ with $a \in A$ and $u = wu_{n+1} = wau'$. We note that by definition of u_{n+1}, $u'\alpha \nsubseteq u_{n+1}\alpha$ which shows that a is not a letter of u'. We shall show that $w \sim_n vw$. Let x be a subword of vw of length less than or equal to n. Then xa is a subword of length less than or equal to $n + 1$ of vwa and therefore vu. Since $u \sim_{n+1} vu$, xa is a subword of $u = wau'$ and, since a is not a letter of u', xa is a subword of wa. Therefore x is a subword of w.

Conversely, it is clear that every subword of w is a subword of vw, and therefore $w \sim_n vw$ as stated. From the inductive hypothesis, there exist $u_1 \ldots u_n \in A^*$ such that $u_1 \ldots u_n = w$ and $v\alpha \subset u_1\alpha \subset \ldots \subset u_n\alpha$. Now $u = wu_{n+1}$ and $u_n\alpha \subset u\alpha = u_{n+1}\alpha$, which concludes the induction.

We shall show that the condition is sufficient, again by induction on n. For $n = 1$, $u_1 = u$ and $v\alpha \subset u\alpha$ implies $u\alpha = (vu)\alpha$, i.e. $u \sim_1 vu$. Suppose that $u = u_1 \ldots u_{n+1}$ with $v\alpha \subset u_1\alpha \subset \ldots \subset u_{n+1}\alpha$. Then $(vu)\alpha = u\alpha = u_{n+1}\alpha$ and $u_1 \ldots u_n \sim_n vu_1 \ldots u_n$ from the inductive hypothesis. Let x be a non-empty subword of length less than or equal to $n + 1$ of vu. Let x' be the longest right factor of x such that x is a subword of u_{n+1} and put $x = x''x'$ (Fig. 1).

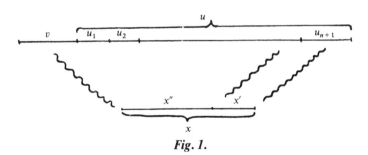

Fig. 1.

Since $(vu)\alpha = u_{n+1}\alpha$, the factor u_{n+1} contains all the letters of vu, and therefore of x, at least once and consequently x' is non-empty. If we take account of the definition of x', x'' is then a subword of length less than or equal to n of $vu_1 \ldots u_n$. Since $u_1 \ldots u_n \sim_n vu_1 \ldots u_n$, x'' is in fact a subword of $u_1 \ldots u_n$ and therefore x is a subword of u. Conversely, every subword of u is clearly a subword of vu and therefore $u \sim_{n+1} vu$, which completes the proof.

Corollary 1.4

For every $u, v \in A^*$, we have $(uv)^n u \sim_n (uv)^n \sim_n v(uv)^n$.

Proof

The formula $(uv)^n \sim_n v(uv)^n$ can be deduced immediately from the preceding proposition. The formula $(uv)^n \sim_n (uv)^n u$ is similar.

In conclusion we give a proposition which presents a remarkable combinatorial property of the congruence $\sim_n$.

Proposition 1.5

If $f \sim_n g$, there exists a word h such that f is a subword of h, g is a subword of h and $f \sim_n h \sim_n g$.

The proof is achieved by induction on $k = |f| + |g| - 2|f \wedge g|$, where $f \wedge g$ is the largest left factor common to f and g. If $k = 0$, then $f = g$ and it suffices to take $h = f = g$. The result is also evident if f is a subword of g (or g is a subword of f). These cases are excluded from now on. Then we have $f = uav$, $g = ubw$ with $a, b \in A$ and $a \neq b$. We shall show that $ubw \sim_n ubav$ or that $uav \sim_n uabw$. Suppose that none of these assertions is true. Since $ubw = g \sim_n f$ and f is a subword of $ubav$, there exists a word r of length less than or equal to n which is a subword of $ubav$ but not of ubw. Likewise there exists a word s of length less than or equal to n which is a subword of $uabw$ but not of uav.

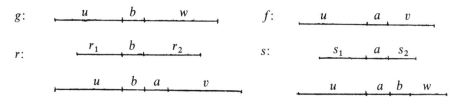

Necessarily $r = r_1 b r_2$ where r_1 is a subword of u and r_2 is a subword of av, and $s = s_1 a s_2$ where s_1 is a subword of u and s_2 is a subword of bw. Hence we can deduce that $r_1 b$ is not a subword of u (for otherwise $r = r_1 b r_2$ would be a subword of $uav = f$ and therefore of g). Likewise $s_1 a$ is not a subword of u.

Since r_2 is a subword of av, we have $r_2 = r_2'' r_2'$ where $r_2'' = 1$ or a and r_2' is a subword of v. Likewise, since s_2 is a subword of bw, we have $s_2 = s_2'' s_2'$ where $s_2'' = 1$ or b and s_2' is a subword of w. Finally

$$|r_1 b s_2'| + |s_1 a r_2'| \leq |r_1 a s_2| + |s_1 b r_2| \leq |r| + |s| \leq 2n$$

and therefore one of the words $r_1 b s_2'$ or $s_1 a r_2'$ is of length less than or equal to n. Suppose for example that this is $r_1 b s_2'$. Then $r_1 b s_2'$ is a subword of $ubw = g$ and therefore also of $f = uav$. However, $r_1 b$ is not a subword of u. Therefore $b s_2'$ is a subword of v,

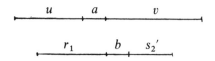

and *a fortiori* s_2 is a subword of v. Thus $s = s_1 a s_2$ is a subword of $uav = f$ — a contradiction. Therefore one of the assertions $ubw \sim_n ubav$ or $uav \sim_n uabw$ stated above is true. Suppose, for example, that $f = uav \sim_n uabw$. Then

$$|uav| + |uabw| - 2|uav \wedge uabw| \leq |f| + |g| + 1 - 2|ua|$$
$$\leq |f| + |g| + 1 - (2|f \wedge g| + 2)$$
$$< k$$

From the inductive hypothesis, there exists h such that $f = uav$ is a subword of h, $uabw$ is a subword of h and $f \sim_n h \sim_n uabw$. The proposition follows from this, since g is a subword of $uabw$.

Example 1.1

Let $f = a^3 b^3 a^3 b^3$ and $g = a^2 b^4 a^4 b^2$. We have $f \sim_4 g$ since all the words of length 4 except *baba* are subwords of f and g. Applying the algorithm described in the proof, we obtain successively

$$f = (aa)a(b^3 a^3 b^3) \sim_4 (aa)b(b^3 a^4 b^2) = g$$

whence

$$(aa)a(b^3 a^3 b^3) \sim_4 (aa)ab(b^3 a^4 b^2) \quad \text{or} \quad (aa)b(b^3 a^4 b^2) \sim_4 (aa)ba(b^3 a^3 b^3)$$

The second possibility can be ruled out, for *baba* is a subword of $a^2 bab^3 a^3 b^3$. Therefore

$$(a^3 b^3)a(a^2 b^3) \sim_4 (a^3 b^3)b(a^4 b^2)$$

and consequently

$$(a^3 b^3)a(a^2 b^3) \sim_4 (a^3 b^3)ab(a^4 b^2) \quad \text{or} \quad (a^3 b^3)b(a^4 b^2) \sim_4 (a^3 b^3)ba(a^2 b^3)$$

The first possibility can be ruled out for *baba* is a subword of $a^3 b^3 aba^4 b^2$. Then

$$(a^3 b^4 a^3)a(b^2) \sim_4 (a^3 b^4 a^3)b(b^2)$$

and consequently

$$(a^3 b^4 a^3)a(b^2) \sim_4 (a^3 b^4 a^3)ab(b^2) \quad \text{or} \quad (a^3 b^4 a^3)b(b^2) \sim_4 (a^3 b^4 a^3)ba(b^2)$$

The second possibility can be ruled out for *baba* is a subword of $a^3 b^4 a^3 bab^2$. Therefore

$$a^3 b^4 a^4 b^2 \sim_4 a^3 b^4 a^4 b^3$$

It follows from this that f and g are subwords of $h = a^3 b^4 a^4 b^3$ and that $f \sim_4 g \sim_4 h$.

We now arrive at the main theorem of this section.

Theorem 1.6 (I. Simon)

A language is piecewise testable if and only if its syntactic monoid is $\mathcal{J}$-trivial.

Corollary 1.7

For every alphabet A, $A^* \mathscr{J}$ is the boolean algebra generated by the languages of the form $A^* a_1 A^* a_2 \ldots A^* a_n A^*$ where the a_i are letters.

Proof

Let L be a piecewise-testable language. Then L is the union of classes modulo $\sim_n$ for a certain $n > 0$ and therefore L is recognized by $A^*/\sim_n$. Now by Corollary 1.4, $A^*/\sim_n$ satisfies the equation $(xy)^n x = (xy)^n = y(xy)^n$ and therefore is $\mathscr{J}$-trivial by Chapter 3, Proposition 4.4. Since $M(L)$ divides $A^*/\sim_n$, $M(L)$ is also $\mathscr{J}$-trivial.

Conversely, let M be a $\mathscr{J}$-trivial monoid and let $L \subset A^*$ be a language recognized by a morphism $A^* \to M$ which we shall denote by $u \to \bar{u}$. We shall show that L is the union of classes modulo $\sim_{2n-1}$ where n is the maximal length of chains of elements of M for the ordering $\leq_{\mathscr{J}}$ (which we shall denote in what follows by $\leq$ for simplicity); in other words n is chosen in such a way that if $m_0 \leq m_1 \ldots \leq m_n$ are elements of M, at least two of them are equal. In fact it is sufficient to verify that if $f \sim_{2n-1} g$, then $\bar{f} = \bar{g}$. Proposition 1.5 enables us to assume that f is a subword of g. We note furthermore that if f is a subword of h and h is a subword of g, we also have $f \sim_{2n-1} h$. This enables us to assume that $f = uv$ and $g = uav$. In this case we have by Proposition 1.2 $ua \sim_n u$ or $av \sim_n v$. Let us take this last case. By Proposition 1.3, there exist $v_1, \ldots, v_n \in A^*$ such that $v = v_1 \ldots v_n$ and $\{a\} \subset v_1 \alpha \subset \ldots \subset v_n \alpha$. Consider the ordered sequence $1 \geq \bar{v}_n \geq \overline{v_{n-1} v_n} \ldots \geq \overline{v_1 \ldots v_n}$. From the choice of n there exists $i < j$ with $\overline{v_i \ldots v_j \ldots v_n} = \overline{v_j \ldots v_n} = s$. Let $b \in v_i \alpha$. Then $v_i = v_i' b v_i''$ and we have $\overline{v_i \ldots v_n} \leq \overline{b v_i'' \ldots v_n} \leq \overline{v_i'' \ldots v_n} \leq \overline{v_j \ldots v_n}$, whence $\overline{v_i \ldots v_n} = \overline{b v_j \ldots v_n} = \overline{v_j \ldots v_n}$. Consequently, we have $\bar{b} s = s$ for all $b \in v_i \alpha$ and therefore $\bar{v} = \overline{v_1 \ldots v_n} = \overline{a v_1 \ldots v_n} = \overline{av}$. From this we can deduce $\bar{g} = \overline{uav} = \overline{uv} = \bar{f}$ which completes the proof.

Simon's theorem has unexpected consequences which we shall now examine in detail. We start by defining, for each integer $n > 0$, three monoids $\mathscr{C}_n$, $\mathscr{R}_n$ and $\mathscr{U}_n$ which will serve us as examples of $\mathscr{J}$-trivial monoids.

$\mathscr{C}_n$ is the submonoid of $\mathscr{T}_n$ formed by **increasing** and **extensive** functions from $\{1, \ldots, n\}$ into itself, i.e. functions f such that

(a) if $1 \leq i \leq j \leq n$, then $if \leq jf$
(b) if $1 \leq i \leq n$, then $i \leq if$

$\mathscr{R}_n$ denotes the monoid of **reflexive** relations on the set $\{1, \ldots, n\}$. It is convenient to consider $\mathscr{R}_n$ as a monoid of matrices. For this we associate with each relation R on $\{1, \ldots, n\}$ a boolean matrix (i.e. a matrix with entries 0 or 1) $((R_{ij}))_{1 \leq i,j \leq n}$ defined by

$R_{ij} = 1$ if $(i,j) \in R$
$R_{ij} = 0$ otherwise

If R and S are two relations, we can verify that

$$(RS)_{ij} = \sum_{1 \le k \le n} R_{ik} S_{kj}$$

where the sum and the product are *boolean*, i.e. they are governed by the formulae

$$1 + 1 = 1 + 0 = 0 + 1 = 1 \qquad\qquad 0 + 0 = 0$$
$$0.0 = 0.1 = 1.0 = 0 \qquad\qquad 1.1 = 1$$

In other words, the matrix associated with the relation RS is the **boolean product** of the matrices representing R and S.

This implies that $\mathcal{R}_n$ can be identified with the set of boolean matrices of size $n \times n$ whose diagonal elements are all equal to 1. For example

$$\mathcal{R}_2 = \left\{ \begin{pmatrix} 1 & 0 \\ 0 & 1 \end{pmatrix}, \begin{pmatrix} 1 & 1 \\ 0 & 1 \end{pmatrix}, \begin{pmatrix} 1 & 0 \\ 1 & 1 \end{pmatrix}, \begin{pmatrix} 1 & 1 \\ 1 & 1 \end{pmatrix} \right\}$$

$\mathcal{U}_n$ is the submonoid of $\mathcal{R}_n$ consisting of the upper triangular matrices of $\mathcal{R}_n$. The matrices of $\mathcal{U}_n$ are called **unitriangular**. For example

$$\mathcal{U}_3 = \left\{ \begin{pmatrix} 1 & \varepsilon_1 & \varepsilon_2 \\ 0 & 1 & \varepsilon_3 \\ 0 & 0 & 1 \end{pmatrix} \middle| \ \varepsilon_1, \varepsilon_2, \varepsilon_3 = 0 \quad \text{or} \quad 1 \right\}$$

We then have the following result.

Proposition 1.8
For every integer $n > 0$, the monoids $\mathcal{C}_n$, $\mathcal{R}_n$ and $\mathcal{U}_n$ are $\mathcal{J}$-trivial.

Proof
We shall show first that $\mathcal{C}_n$ is $\mathcal{J}$-trivial. If $f, g \in \mathcal{C}_n$ and $f \mathcal{J} g$, there exist $a, b, c, d \in \mathcal{C}_n$ such that $g = afb$ and $f = cgd$. Let $i \in \{1, \dots, n\}$. Since a is extensive we have $i \le ia$, and since f is increasing we have $if \le iaf$. Then, since b is extensive, it follows that $iaf \le iafb$ and finally $if \le iafb = ig$. Similar reasoning would show that $ig \le if$. Hence we can deduce that $f = g$ and $\mathcal{C}_n$ is $\mathcal{J}$-trivial.

Since $\mathcal{U}_n$ is a submonoid of $\mathcal{R}_n$, it is sufficient to establish that $\mathcal{R}_n$ is $\mathcal{J}$-trivial. Let $R, S \in \mathcal{R}_n$ and suppose $R \mathcal{J} S$. Then there exist $A, B, C, D \in \mathcal{R}_n$ such that $S = ARB$ and $R = CSD$. Therefore if $(i,j) \in R$ we have also $(i,j) \in S = ARB$ since $(i,i) \in A$ and $(j,j) \in B$. Likewise, $(i,j) \in S$ implies $(i,j) \in R$ and therefore $R = S$. Consequently $\mathcal{R}_n$ is $\mathcal{J}$-trivial.

The following is another elementary property of the monoids $\mathcal{C}_n$, $\mathcal{R}_n$ and $\mathcal{U}_n$.

Proposition 1.9
For every integer $n, m > 0$, $\mathcal{C}_n \times \mathcal{C}_m$, $\mathcal{R}_n \times \mathcal{R}_m$ or $\mathcal{U}_n \times \mathcal{U}_m$ divides $\mathcal{C}_{n+m}$, $\mathcal{R}_{n+m}$ or $\mathcal{U}_{n+m}$ respectively.

Proof

Let $\varphi : \mathscr{C}_n \times \mathscr{C}_m \to \mathscr{C}_{n+m}$ be the function defined by $(f, g)\varphi = h$ where

$$ih = if \quad \text{if} \quad 1 \le i \le n$$
$$ih = (i - n)g + n \quad \text{if} \quad n + 1 \le i \le n + m$$

φ is clearly an injective morphism and therefore $\mathscr{C}_n \times \mathscr{C}_m$ divides $\mathscr{C}_{n+m}$. Let $\psi : \mathscr{R}_n \times \mathscr{R}_m \to \mathscr{R}_{n+m}$ be the function defined by $(R, S)\psi = T$ where T is the relation defined by

$$(i, j) \in T \text{ if and only if } (i, j) \in R \text{ or } (i - n, j - n) \in S$$

Then ψ is an injective morphism and therefore $\mathscr{R}_n \times \mathscr{R}_m$ divides $\mathscr{R}_{n+m}$. The proof is similar for $\mathscr{U}_n$.

The statement which follows is a representation theorem for $\mathscr{J}$-trivial monoids, due to H. Straubing. Another representation theorem has been recently proved by H. Straubing and D. Thérien by direct algebraic methods, leading to a new proof of Simon's theorem.

Theorem 1.10

Let M be a finite monoid. The following conditions are equivalent.

(1) M is $\mathscr{J}$-trivial.
(2)   There exists an integer $n > 0$ such that M divides $\mathscr{C}_n$.
(3)   There exists an integer $n > 0$ such that M divides $\mathscr{R}_n$.
(4)   There exists an integer $n > 0$ such that M divides $\mathscr{U}_n$.

Proof

By Proposition 1.8 the monoids $\mathscr{C}_n$, $\mathscr{R}_n$ and $\mathscr{U}_n$ are $\mathscr{J}$-trivial. Therefore one of the conditions (2), (3) or (4) implies (1). Moreover (4) implies (3) since $\mathscr{U}_n$ is a submonoid of $\mathscr{R}_n$. It remains then to prove that (1) implies (2) and (4).

Let M be a $\mathscr{J}$-trivial monoid. By Chapter 2, Proposition 2.3, there exist a finite alphabet A and languages $L_1, \ldots, L_k \in A^* \mathscr{J}$ such that M divides $M(L_1) \times \ldots \times M(L_k)$. Now by Corollary 1.7, each language L_i is in the boolean algebra generated by the languages of the form $A^* a_1 A^* a_2 \ldots A^* a_r A^*$ (where the a_j are letters). Hence we can deduce, taking account of Chapter 1, Corollary 2.8, that M divides a product of monoids of the form $M(A^* a_1 A^* a_2 \ldots A^* a_r A^*)$. It is sufficient then, by Proposition 1.9, to prove that, if $L = A^* a_1 A^* a_2 \ldots A^* a_r A^*$, then $M(L)$ divides $\mathscr{C}_n$ (or $\mathscr{U}_n$) for a certain integer $n > 0$. Now a small calculation (based on the fact that $A^* a_1 A^* a_2 \ldots A^* a_r A^* = (A \backslash \{a_1\})^* a_1 (A \backslash \{a_2\})^* a_2 \ldots a_r A^*$ enables us to see that the minimal automaton of L is $\mathscr{A} = (Q, A, \cdot)$ with $Q = \{1, \ldots, r + 1\}$ and

$$i \cdot a = i \qquad \text{if} \quad a \ne a_i$$
$$i \cdot a = i + 1 \quad \text{if} \quad a = a_i$$

This automaton is represented by the diagram below where, conventionally, all the transitions of the type $i \cdot a = i$ (for $a \neq a_i$) are represented by one and the same arrow from i to i labelled by $A \backslash \{a_i\}$:

Since the transitions of $\mathcal{A}$ are increasing and extensive functions, the transition monoid of $\mathcal{A}$ —which is also the syntactic monoid of L— is a submonoid of $\mathscr{C}_{r+1}$, which establishes that (1) implies (2).

Moreover L is also recognized by $\mathscr{U}_{r+1}$. In fact let $\mu : A^* \to \mathscr{U}_{r+1}$ be the morphism defined by

$$(a\mu)_{i,j} = 1 \quad \text{if } i = j$$
$$= 1 \quad \text{if } i + 1 = j \text{ and } a = a_i$$
$$= 0 \quad \text{in the other cases}$$

and let P be the set of matrices of $\mathscr{U}_{r+1}$ such that $m_{1,r+1} = 1$. We can establish then that $L = P\mu^{-1}$ and therefore $\mathscr{U}_{r+1}$ recognizes L (the details are left as an exercise for the reader). Consequently $M(L)$ divides $\mathscr{U}_{r+1}$. For the reader familiar with the theory of automata, the preceding argument amounts to saying that L is recognized by the following non-deterministic automaton:

2. Star-free languages; Schützenberger's theorem

We shall prove in this section a fundamental result in the theory of languages which is due to Schützenberger. This theorem describes the variety of languages corresponding to the variety of monoids A.

We saw in the first chapter that rational languages could be expressed starting from letters of the alphabet with the help of the boolean operations product and star. If we suppress this last operation we obtain the 'star-free' languages, of which the following is the precise definition.

Definition 2.1

Let A be a finite alphabet. The set of star-free languages of A^* is the smallest set $A^*\mathscr{S}$ of languages of A^* such that

(a)   for every word $u \in A^*$, $\{u\} \in A^*\mathscr{S}$
(b) $A^*\mathscr{S}$ is closed under finite boolean operations and concatenation product

We give immediately some examples of star-free languages over the alphabet $A = \{a, b\}$. The empty language A^* and, more generally, finite or cofinite languages are star-free languages. Piecewise-testable languages are star free since they are boolean combinations of languages of the form $A^*a_1 A^*a_2 \ldots a_r A^*$. Despite appearances the language $(ab)^*$ is also a star-free language since

$$(ab)^* = A^* \backslash (bA^* \cup A^*a \cup A^*aaA^* \cup A^*bbA^*)$$

In contrast, we shall see that the language $(aa)^*$ is not star free. This is an immediate consequence of Schützenberger's theorem.

Theorem 2.1 (Schützenberger)

A recognizable language is star free if and only if its syntactic monoid is aperiodic.

We immediately express this statement in terms of varieties.

Corollary 2.2

Let $\mathscr{A}$ be the variety of languages corresponding to A. Then for every alphabet $A, A^*\mathscr{A}$ is the set of star-free languages of A.

The proof of Schützenberger's theorem is rather long. We shall first establish the inclusion $A^*\mathscr{S} \subset A^*\mathscr{A}$ with the help of the following result.

Proposition 2.3 (Straubing)

Let X and Y be two recognizable languages of A^*. Then there exists an aperiodic relational morphism

$$\tau : M(XY) \to M(X) \times M(Y)$$

Proof

Let us write $\eta_X : A^* \to M(X)$, $\eta_Y : A^* \to M(Y)$ and $\eta : A^* \to M(XY)$ for the respective syntactic morphisms of X, Y and XY. Since η is a surjective morphism, $\eta^{-1} : M(XY) \to A^*$ is a relational morphism and therefore $\tau = \eta^{-1}(\eta_X \times \eta_Y) : M(XY) \to M(X) \times M(Y)$ is a relational morphism.

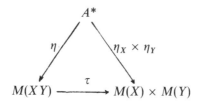

Let us write $\sim_X$, $\sim_Y$ and $\sim$ for the syntactic equivalences defined by the languages X, Y and XY respectively and let $e = (e_1, e_2)$ be an idempotent of $M(X) \times M(Y)$. If $g \in e(\eta_X \times \eta_Y)^{-1}$, we have in particular $g \sim_X g^2$ and $g \sim_Y g^2$. Let $n \geq 2$ and $u, v \in A^*$. If $ug^n v \in XY$, we can write $ug^n v = xy$ with $x \in X$ and $y \in Y$.

Two cases are possible. Either $x = ugx_1$ with $x_1 y = g^{n-1}v$, or $y = y_1 gv$ with $xy_1 = ug^{n-1}$. Let us consider the first case (the other case is similar). It follows, since $g \sim_X g^2$, that $ug^2 x_1 \in X$, whence $ug^2 x_1 y = ug^{n+1}v \in XY$. Therefore, for $n \geq 2$, $ug^n v \in XY$ implies $ug^{n+1}v \in XY$. A similar argument shows that, for $n \geq 3$, $ug^{n+1}v \in XY$ implies $ug^n v \in XY$. In particular $g^3 \sim g^4$ which shows that $e\tau^{-1}$ is aperiodic. Therefore, from Chapter 3, Proposition 5.7, τ is an aperiodic relational morphism.

Let us return to the inclusion $A^*\mathscr{S} \subset A^*\mathscr{A}$. First of all, by definition of a variety of languages, $A^*\mathscr{A}$ is closed under finite boolean operations. Moreover, $A^*\mathscr{A}$ is closed under the product operation: if $X, Y \in A^*\mathscr{A}$, we have $M(X), M(Y) \in A$ by definition and, from Proposition 2.3, there exists an aperiodic relational morphism $\tau: M(XY) \to M(X) \times M(Y)$. It follows from this that $M(XY) \in A$, whence $XY \in A^*\mathscr{A}$. It remains to verify that $A^*\mathscr{A}$ contains languages of the type $\{u\}$ where $u \in A^*$. Since $A^*\mathscr{A}$ is closed under concatenation product it is sufficient to verify that $\{1\} \in A^*\mathscr{A}$ and that $\{a\} \in A^*\mathscr{A}$ for every $a \in A$. Now the calculation shows that $M\{a\} = \mathbb{Z}_{1,2}$ is aperiodic and therefore $\{a\} \in A^*\mathscr{A}$. Finally, since varieties of languages are closed under left quotient, we have $\{1\} = a^{-1}\{a\} \in A^*\mathscr{A}$. Therefore $A^*\mathscr{S} \subset A^*\mathscr{A}$.

Conversely, we shall show by induction on card(M) that every language of A^* recognized by an aperiodic monoid M is in $A^*\mathscr{S}$. We shall denote by $A^*\triangle M$ the set of languages of A^* recognized by a strict divisor of M. The inductive hypothesis will then be on the sequence $A^*\triangle M \subset A^*\mathscr{S}$.

If card$(M) = 1$, the only languages of A^* recognized by M are A^* and $\varnothing$ which are in $A^*\mathscr{S}$ by definition.

If card$(M) = 2$, M is necessarily equal to U_1 which is the only aperiodic with two elements. By Chapter 2, Proposition 3.10, the languages of A^* recognized by U_1 are in the boolean algebra generated by the languages of the form A^*aA^* where $a \in A$. In particular these languages are in $A^*\mathscr{S}$.

Suppose that card$(M) \geq 3$ and let L be a language recognized by M. Then there exist a morphism $\eta: A^* \to M$ and a subset P of M such that $L = P\eta^{-1}$. We can assume that η is surjective for otherwise the inductive hypothesis could be applied since L would be recognized by $A^*\eta$, a *proper* submonoid of M. Furthermore, we have

$$P\eta^{-1} = \bigcup_{m \in P} m\eta^{-1}$$

which enables us to return to the case where $L = m\eta^{-1}$ with $m \in M$.

We shall denote by K the intersection of the ideals of M having at least two elements. K is itself an ideal, and therefore a semigroup. Its structure is made precise in the following lemma.

Lemma 2.4

(1) If M does not possess a zero, K is the minimal ideal of M; it is therefore a simple idempotent semigroup.

(2) If M possesses a zero, denoted by 0, then $D = K\backslash 0$ is either empty or a $\mathscr{D}$-class of M and K is 0-simple or has zero square (i.e. $K^2 = 0$).

Proof

(1) If M does not possess a zero, the minimal ideal contains at least two elements and is therefore equal to K.

(2) Let $x, y \in D = K\backslash 0$. Then $I = MxM$ is an ideal containing at least two elements, x and 0. Therefore $K \subset I$ and $y \in I$. Likewise we have $x \in MyM$ and consequently $x \mathscr{J} y$. Therefore D is a $\mathscr{D}$-class. If $K^2 \neq 0$, there exist $x, y \in D$ such that $xy \in D$. We then have $xy \in R_x \cap L_y$ by Chapter 3, Proposition 1.4(2), and D is regular by Chapter 3, Propositions 1.6 and 1.9. Now, by Chapter 3, Proposition 1.10, all the elements of D are $\mathscr{D}$-equivalent *in* K and by Chapter 3, Proposition 3.1, K is 0-simple.

We return to the proof of the theorem.

Case (i) : $m \notin K$ In this case there exists by definition of K an ideal I — having at least two elements — which does not contain m. If φ denotes the morphism of M onto M/I, we have $m = m\varphi\varphi^{-1}$ and consequently $m\eta^{-1} = (m\varphi)(\eta\varphi)^{-1}$. It follows from this that $m\eta^{-1}$ is recognized by M/I and therefore $L \in A^*\triangle M$. We reach the conclusion from the inductive hypothesis.

Case (ii) : M has a zero and $m = 0$ Let C be the set of letters of A whose image under η is the zero of M. Formally $C = \{a \in A \,|\, a\eta = 0\}$. We shall establish the formula

$$0\eta^{-1} = A^*CA^* \cup \bigcup_{(a,n,a')\in E} A^*a(n\eta^{-1})a'A^* \tag{1}$$

where

$$E = \{(a, n, a')\,|\,a, a' \in A\backslash C, n \in M\backslash K \text{ and } (a\eta)n(a'\eta) = 0 \quad (a\eta)n \neq 0 \quad n(a'\eta) \neq 0\}$$

The inclusion from right to left follows immediately from the definitions of C and E: we have $(A^*CA^*)\eta = M(C\eta)M \subset 0$ and if $(a, n, a') \in E$ $(A^*a(n\eta^{-1})a'A^*)\eta = M(a\eta)n(a'\eta)M = 0$. To prove the opposite inclusion let us consider a word $f \in 0\eta^{-1}\backslash A^*CA^* = 0\eta^{-1} \cap (A\backslash C)^*$. Since M has at least two elements, we have $1 \neq 0$ in M and therefore f is not the empty word. Consequently f admits a longer left factor g such that $g\eta \neq 0$, and we can deduce from this a factorization $f = ga'g'$ with $a' \in A\backslash C$, $g' \in (A\backslash C)^*$ and $(ga')\eta = 0$. Since $a'\eta \neq 0$, the word g admits a longer right factor h such that $(ha')\eta \neq 0$ and a factorization $g = h'ah$ where $h' \in (A\backslash C)^*$, $a \in A\backslash C$ and $(aha')\eta = 0$. Since $g\eta \neq 0$, we have also $(ah)\eta \neq 0$. Put $n = h\eta$. If $n \in K$, we have, since $(ah)\eta \neq 0$ and $(ha')\eta \neq 0$, $n \mathscr{R} n(a'\eta)$ and $(a\eta)n \mathscr{L} n$. Since $D = K\backslash 0$ is a $\mathscr{D}$-class, Green's lemma implies $(a\eta)n(a'\eta) \in D$ which contradicts the fact that $(aha')\eta = 0$. It is therefore true that $n \notin K$ and we have

$f \in A^*a(n\eta^{-1})a'A^*$ with $(a, n, a') \in E$, which establishes formula (1).

Since $n \notin K$, we have $n\eta^{-1} \in A^* \triangle M$ from case (i) and therefore $n\eta^{-1} \in A^*\mathcal{S}$ by the inductive hypothesis. Consequently from (1) we have also $0\eta^{-1} \in A^*\mathcal{S}$ since $A^*\mathcal{S}$ is closed under boolean operations and concatenation product.

Case (iii): $m \in K\backslash 0 (= K$ *if K has no zero*) By Lemma 2.3, $K\backslash 0$ is in all cases a $\mathcal{D}$-class. By the results in Chapter 3 we have $H_m = R_m \cap I_m$ and since M is aperiodic, and therefore $\mathcal{H}$-trivial, we also have $H_m = \{m\}$. Finally all the elements of mM are in K and are therefore, with the exception of the zero, in the $\mathcal{R}$-class of m. Hence we deduce that $R_m = mM\backslash 0$ and finally

$$\{m\} = (mM \cap Mm)\backslash 0 \tag{2}$$

Of course this formula becomes $\{m\} = mM \cap Mm$ if M has no zero. From (2) it is sufficient to prove that $(mM)\eta^{-1}$ and $(Mm)\eta^{-1}$ are in $A^*\mathcal{S}$. Now we have

$$(mM)\eta^{-1} = 0\eta^{-1} \cup \bigcup_{(n,a)\in F} (n\eta^{-1})aA^* \tag{3}$$

with

$$F = \{(n, a) \mid n \in M\backslash K, a \in A \text{ and } n(a\eta) \in R_m\}$$

The inclusion from the right to the left follows immediately from the definitions. To establish the opposite inclusion, let us consider a word $f \in (mM)\eta^{-1}$. If $f\eta = 0$, we have $f \in 0\eta^{-1}$. If not, $f\eta \in R_m$ and as $1 \notin K$ (for M has at least two elements) we have *a fortiori* $1\eta = 1 \notin R_m$. The word f then admits a larger left factor g such that $g\eta \notin R_m$. Hence we deduce that there is a factorization $f = gag'$ with $n = g\eta \notin R_m$, $n(a\eta) \in R_m$, $a \in A$ and $g, g' \in A^*$. Moreover $n \notin K$ for, if $n \in K$, we find on the one hand $n \leq_{\mathcal{J}} m$, since $K = MmM$, and on the other hand $m \leq_{\mathcal{R}} n$, since $n(a\eta) \in R_m$, whence finally $n \mathcal{R} m$ and $n \in R_m$. Therefore we have $(n, a) \in F$ and $f \in (n\eta^{-1})aA^*$, which establishes the equality (3).

Since $n \notin K$, we have $n\eta^{-1} \in A^*\triangle M$ from case (i), whence $n\eta^{-1} \in A^*\mathcal{S}$ by induction and finally $(mM)\eta^{-1} \in A^*\mathcal{S}$ from (3). The proof for $(Mm)\eta^{-1}$ is similar, which completes the induction.

Example 2.1

Let $A = \{a, b\}$ and $L = \{ab, ba\}^+$. The minimal automaton of this language is represented in Fig. 2.

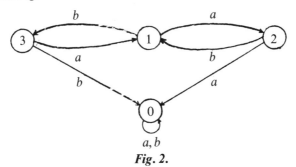

a, b

Fig. 2.

The calculation of the syntactic monoid of L and its $\mathscr{D}$-classes structure are given below.

	1	2	3	0
a	2	0	1	0
b	3	1	0	0
a^2	0	0	2	0
* ab	1	0	3	0
* ba	1	2	0	0
b^2	0	3	0	0
· a^3	0	0	0	0
a^2b	0	0	1	0
ab^2	3	0	0	0
ba^2	2	0	0	0
b^2a	0	1	0	0
a^2b^2	0	0	3	0
ab^2a	1	0	0	0
b^2a^2	0	2	0	0

Relations

$$aba = a \qquad bab = b \qquad b^3 = a^3 = 0 \qquad ba^2b = ab^2a$$
$$a^2b^2a = a^2b \qquad ab^2a^2 = ba^2$$

$$\boxed{*\ 1}$$

	012	013
03/1/2	* ba	b
1/02/3	a	* ab

	01	02	03
023/1	* ab^2a	ba^2	ab^2
013/2	b^2a	* b^2a^2	b^2
012/3	a^2b	a^2	* a^2b^2

$$\boxed{*\ 0}$$

Applying Schützenberger's algorithm, we obtain the following star-free expression for L:

$$L = \{1\} \cup (ab)^+ \cup (ba)^+ \cup [((ba)^+ aA^* \cup (ab)^+ bA^*) \cap (A^*a(ab)^+ \cup A^*b(ba)^+)]$$
$$\setminus (A^*a(ab)^*a(ba)^*aA^* \cup A^*b(ba)^*b(ab)^*bA^*)$$

where

$$(ab)^+ = (aA^* \cap A^*b) \setminus (A^*aaA^* \cup A^*bbA^*)$$

and

$$(ba)^+ = (bA^* \cap A^*a) \setminus (A^*aaA^* \cup A^*bbA^*)$$

3. $\mathscr{R}$-trivial and $\mathscr{L}$-trivial languages

In the two preceding sections we have described languages whose syntactic monoid is $\mathscr{J}$-trivial and $\mathscr{H}$-trivial (i.e. aperiodic, by Chapter 3, Proposition 4.2). We shall now describe the languages whose syntactic monoids are $\mathscr{R}$-trivial and $\mathscr{L}$-trivial. Curiously, the proofs of these results are distinctly easier than those of the theorems of Simon and Schützenberger. The proof which we give here uses automata. We could give other proofs inspired by Simon's theorem (the method of congruences) or by Schützenberger's theorem (induction on the cardinal number of the syntactic monoid) or by algorithms for the decomposition of recognizable languages (see Eilenberg, *Automata, Languages and Machines*, Vol. B, Chapter 10) or by the theory of the wreath product.

Let $\mathscr{A} = (Q, A, \cdot)$ be a finite automaton. We shall say that $\mathscr{A}$ is **extensive** if there exists a total ordering on Q, denoted by $\leq$, such that for every $q \in Q$ and for every $a \in A$, $q \leq q \cdot a$. We note at once the following proposition.

Proposition 3.1
The transition monoid of an extensive automaton is $\mathscr{R}$-trivial.

Proof
Let $\mathscr{A} = (Q, A, \cdot)$ be an extensive automaton and let u, v, x, y be words of A^*. Suppose that ux and v on the one hand, and vy and u on the other hand, have the same action on Q. It then follows, for every $q \in Q$, that $q \cdot u \leq q \cdot ux = q \cdot v$ and $q \cdot v \leq q \cdot vy = q \cdot u$, whence $q \cdot u = q \cdot v$ and therefore u and v have the same action on Q. It follows from this that the transition monoid of $\mathscr{A}$ is $\mathscr{R}$-trivial.

We can deduce from Proposition 1.1 a first characterization of languages recognized by an $\mathscr{R}$-trivial monoid.

Proposition 3.2
Let L be a recognizable language of A^*. Then L is recognized by a finite $\mathscr{R}$-trivial monoid if and only if L is recognized by an extensive automaton.

Proof

If L is recognized by an extensive automaton $\mathscr{A}$, L is recognized by the monoid $M(\mathscr{A})$ by Chapter 1, Proposition 2.1. Now the latter is $\mathscr{R}$-trivial by Proposition 3.1.

Conversely, suppose that L is recognized by an $\mathscr{R}$-trivial monoid M. Then there exist a morphism $\eta:A^* \to M$ and a subset P of M such that $P\eta^{-1} = M$. Moreover the relation $\leq_{\mathscr{R}}$ is a partial ordering on M and by Chapter 0, Proposition 0.1, there exists a total ordering $\leq$ on M such that $a \leq_{\mathscr{R}} b$ implies $b \leq a$. Consider for the moment the automaton $\mathscr{A} = (M, A, \cdot)$ defined by $m \cdot a = m(a\eta)$. Since $m(a\eta) \leq_{\mathscr{R}} m$, we have $m \leq m \cdot a$ and therefore $\mathscr{A}$ is extensive. Moreover, if we take 1 for the initial state and P for the set of final states, we know that $\mathscr{A}$ recognizes L(see Chapter 1, proof of Proposition 2.1).

We can now describe the variety of languages $\mathscr{R}$ corresponding to $\mathbf{R}$.

Theorem 3.3 (Eilenberg)

For every alphabet A, $A^*\mathscr{R}$ consists of languages which can be written as disjoint unions of languages of the form $A_0^*a_1A_1^*a_2\ldots a_nA_n^*$ where $n \geq 0$, $a_1,\ldots,a_n \in A$, $A_i \subset A \setminus \{a_{i+1}\}$ for $0 \leq i \leq n-1$ and $A_n \subset A$.

Proof

Let $L = A_0^*a_1A_1^*a_2\ldots a_nA_n^*$ with $n \geq 0$, $a_1,\ldots,a_n \in A$ and $A_i \subset A \setminus \{a_{i+1}\}$ for $0 \leq i \leq n-1$. Consider the automaton $\mathscr{A} = (Q, A, \cdot)$ where $Q = \{0, 1, \ldots, n+1\}$ and where for every $a \in A$

$$i \cdot a = \begin{cases} i & \text{if } a \in A_i \\ i+1 & \text{if } a = a_i \\ n+1 & \text{in the other cases} \end{cases} \quad \text{and } (n+1) \cdot a = n+1$$

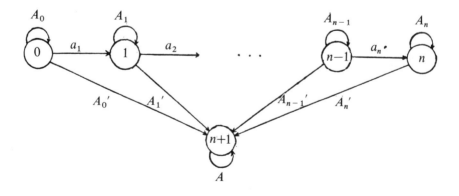

Fig. 3

This automaton is represented by Fig. 3 where we have put A_i' $= A \setminus (A_i \cup \{a_{i+1}\})$.

$\mathscr{A}$ is an extensive automaton which recognizes L if we take 0 as the initial state and $\{n\}$ as the set of final states. We can deduce from Proposition 3.2 that $L \in A^* \mathscr{R}$. As $A^* \mathscr{R}$ is a boolean algebra every union of languages of the same type as L is an element of $A^* \mathscr{R}$.

Conversely, let $K \in A^* \mathscr{R}$. By Proposition 3.2, K is recognized by an extensive automaton $\mathscr{A} = (Q, A, \cdot)$. We can always suppose that $Q = \{1, \ldots, n\}$ and that the ordering on Q is the natural ordering on the integers. K is then a disjoint union of languages of the form $K_{ij} = \{u \in A^* | i \cdot u = j\}$. Let us denote by $S(i,j)$ the set of finite sequences $(i_0, i_1, \ldots, i_k)$ such that $i = i_0 < i_1 < \ldots < i_k = j$. Let us put, for $1 \le p \le q \le n$, $A_{p,q} = \{a \in A | p \cdot a = q\}$ and, if $s = (i_0, i_1, \ldots, i_k) \in S(i,j)$, let us put $K_s = A_{i_0 i_0}{}^* A_{i_0 i_1} A_{i_1 i_1}{}^* \ldots A_{i_{k-1} i_k} A_{i_k i_k}{}^*$. We shall show that

$$K_{ij} = \bigcup_{s \in S(i,j)} K_s$$

First, if $u \in K_s$, we have $i \cdot u = j$ by construction and therefore $u \in K_{i,j}$. Conversely, let $u \in K_{ij}$. If, in the automaton $\mathscr{A}$, we read the word u starting from the state i, we pass successively through the states $i = i_0 < i_1 < \ldots < i_k = j$. For $0 \le p \le k - 1$, let us write a_p for the letter of A such that $i_p \cdot a_p = i_{p+1}$. We define thus a factorization $u = u_0 a_1 u_1 \ldots a_k u_k$ where, for $1 \le p \le k$, $a_p \in A_{i_p i_{p+1}}$ and, for $0 \le p \le k$, $u_p \in A_{i_p i_p}{}^*$. Consequently $u \in K_s$ where $s = (i_0, i_1, \ldots, i_k)$. Moreover, since the reading of the word u determines uniquely the states $i_0, i_1, \ldots, i_k$, we have $u \notin K_t$ if $t \ne s$. Consequently the union

$$\bigcup_{s \in S(i,j)} K_s$$

is disjoint. To conclude the proof, it remains to observe that, if $s = (i_0, i_1, \ldots, i_k)$, K_s is the disjoint union of the languages $A_{i_0 i_0}{}^* a_1 A_{i_1 i_1}{}^* a_2 \ldots a_k A_{i_k i_k}{}^*$ where, for $1 \le p \le k$, a_p runs through $A_{i_{p-1} i_p}$.

We can describe in the same way the variety of languages $\mathscr{R}^t$ corresponding to $\mathbf{R}^r$.

Theorem 3.4

For every alphabet A, $A^* \mathscr{R}^t$ consists of languages which can be written as a disjoint union of languages of the form $A_0{}^* a_1 A_1{}^* a_2 \ldots a_n A_n{}^*$ where $n \ge 0$, $a_1, \ldots, a_n \in A$, $A_0 \subset A$ and, for $1 \le i \le n$, $A_i \subset A \setminus \{a_i\}$.

To conclude this section we note a representation theorem for $\mathscr{R}$-trivial monoids which could be compared with Theorem 1.10. We denote by $\mathscr{E}_n$ the submonoid of $\mathscr{T}_n$ consisting of extensive functions from $\{1, \ldots, n\}$ into itself.

Proposition 3.5

For every $n > 0$, the monoid $\mathscr{E}_n$ is $\mathscr{R}$-trivial.

Proof

Let $f, g \in \mathscr{E}_n$ be such that $f \mathscr{R} g$. There exist $a, b \in \mathscr{E}_n$ such that $fa = g$ and $gb = f$. Let $i \in \{1, \dots, n\}$. Since a is extensive we have $if \leq ifa = ig$ and likewise $ig \leq igb = if$. It follows from this that $if = ig$ for every $i \in \{1, \dots, n\}$, whence $f = g$. Therefore $\mathscr{E}_n$ is $\mathscr{R}$-trivial.

Theorem 3.6
Let M be a finite monoid. The following conditions are equivalent.

(1) M is $\mathscr{R}$-trivial
(2)   There exists an integer $n > 0$ such that M is a submonoid of $\mathscr{E}_n$

Proof

If M is $\mathscr{R}$-trivial, the relation $\leq_{\mathscr{R}}$ is a partial ordering. By Chapter 0, Proposition 0.1, there exists a total ordering $\leq$ on M such that $a \leq_{\mathscr{R}} b$ implies $b \leq a$. It follows from this that, for each $m \in M$, the function $\rho_m : M \to M$ defined by $u \rho_m = um$ is an extensive function (relative to the ordering $\leq$), since $um \leq_{\mathscr{R}} u$ implies $u \leq um = u \rho_m$. Now we have seen (Chapter 1, Proposition 1.5) that the function $m \to \rho_m$ is an injective morphism from M into $\mathscr{T}(M)$. Therefore M is a submonoid of $\mathscr{E}_n$ with $n = \operatorname{card}(M)$.

Conversely, suppose that M is a submonoid of $\mathscr{E}_n$. Then $\mathscr{E}_n$ is $\mathscr{R}$-trivial from Proposition 3.5 and M is also $\mathscr{R}$-trivial since the $\mathscr{R}$-trivial monoids form a variety of monoids.

Problems

Section 1

1.1   Show that every finite (or cofinite) language is piecewise testable.

1.2   (a) Let $A = \{a, b\}$. Show that the language A^*abA^* is piecewise testable.
(b) Let $A = \{a, b, c\}$. Show that the language A^*abA^* is not piecewise testable.

1.3   Let A be a finite alphabet, $a_1, \dots, a_n$ letters of A and $A_0, A_1, \dots, A_n$ subsets of A. Show that if, for $1 \leq i \leq n$, a_i is not an element of A_{i-1}, nor of A_i, then the language $A_0^*a_1 A_1^*a_2 \dots a_n A_n$ is piecewise testable.

1.4   Let M be a finite monoid. Denote by $\mathscr{P}_1(M)$ the monoid of subsets of M containing 1. ($\mathscr{P}_1(M)$ is then a submonoid of the monoid $\mathscr{P}(M)$ (see Chapter 3, Problem 5.3).) Show that $\mathscr{P}_1(M)$ is $\mathscr{J}$-trivial.

1.5   For every word u, v of A^* denote by $\binom{v}{u}$ the number of distinct factorizations of the form $v = v_0 a_1 v_1 \dots a_n v_n$ such that $v_0, \dots, v_n \in A^*$, $a_1, \dots, a_n \in A$ and $a_1 \dots a_n = u$. For example

$$\binom{abab}{ab} = 3 \qquad \binom{aabbaa}{aba} = 8$$

We say that $\binom{v}{u}$ is the binomial coefficient of u and v. Establish the following formulae, where $a, b \in A$ and $u, v, v_1, v_2 \in A^*$:

(1) $\displaystyle \binom{a^p}{a^q} = \binom{p}{q} = \frac{p!}{q!(p-q)!}$

(2) $\displaystyle \binom{a}{u} = \begin{cases} 1 & \text{if } u = a \text{ or } u = 1 \\ 0 & \text{otherwise} \end{cases}$

(3) $\displaystyle \binom{1}{u} = \begin{cases} 1 & \text{if } u = 1 \\ 0 & \text{otherwise} \end{cases}$

(4) $\displaystyle \binom{ua}{vb} = \binom{u}{vb} + \delta_{a,b}\binom{u}{v} \text{ where } \delta_{a,b} = \begin{cases} 1 & \text{if } a = b \\ 0 & \text{otherwise} \end{cases}$

(5) $\displaystyle \binom{v_1 v_2}{u} = \sum_{u = u_1 u_2} \binom{v_1}{u_1}\binom{v_2}{u_2}$

1.6 Let p be a prime number. We recall that a p-group is a finite group whose order is a power of p. Show that the p-groups form a variety G_p. Let $\mathscr{G}_p$ be the corresponding variety of languages. Show that for every alphabet A, $A^*\mathscr{G}_p$ is the boolean algebra generated by the languages

$$ L_{u,i} = \left\{ v \in A^* \middle| \binom{v}{u} \equiv i \bmod p \right\} $$

for $0 \le i < p$ and $u \in A^*$. (Eilenberg and Schützenberger.)

1.7 Let p be a prime number and let A be a finite alphabet. Let A^* be equipped with the coarsest topology which will make continuous all morphisms from A^* into a p-group (provided with the discrete topology).
(a) Prove that for every word $u \in A^*$

$$ \lim_{n \to \infty} u^{n!} = 1 $$

(b) Let L be a recognizable language of A^*. Prove that L is open and closed if and only if $L \in A^*\mathscr{G}_p$.
(c) Prove that the languages of the form $A^*a_1 A^*a_2 \ldots a_n A^*$ (where $n \ge 0$ and $a_1, \ldots, a_n \in A$) are open.

1.8 Prove that a finite $\mathscr{J}$-trivial monoid admits a unique minimal set of generators. (Doyen.)

Section 2
2.1 Let $A = \{a, b\}$. Prove that the languages D_n, defined inductively by $D_0 = \{1\}$ and $D_{n+1} = (aD_n b)^*$, are star-free languages. Give a star-free expression for D_2.

Section 3

3.1 Rework Problem 1.3 using the results of Section 3.

3.2 (Brzozowski–Fich)   Let $n \geq 0$. We define a relation $\equiv_n$ on A^* by $x \equiv_n y$ if and only if the following hold.
  (a) For every prefix u of x, there exists a prefix v of y such that $u \sim_n v$.
  (b) For every prefix v of y, there exists a prefix u of x such that $u \sim_n v$.

  (1) Show that $\equiv_n$ is a congruence with finite index on A^*.
  (2) Show that for every $x, y \in A^*$
      (i) $x \equiv_n y$ implies $x \sim_n y$
      (ii) $x^n \equiv_n x^{n+1}$
      (iii) $(xy)^n \equiv_n (xy)^n x$
  (3) Show that each class modulo $\equiv_n$ contains a unique element of minimal length.
  (4) (This question uses sequential functions which will be defined in the next chapter.) Let $\sigma : A^* \to A^*$ be the function which associates with each word u of A^* the shortest word congruent to u modulo $\equiv_n$. Show that σ is a sequential function realized by the transducer $\mathscr{T} = (Q, A, A, \cdot, *)$ where Q is the set of sets of words of length less than or equal to n and where the transitions are given by the formula (where $P \in Q$ and $a \in A$)

$$P \cdot a = \{v \in A^* \mid |v| \leq n \text{ and } v \text{ is a subword of } ua \text{ for a certain } u \in P\}$$

and the outputs are given by

$$P * a = \begin{cases} a & \text{if } P \cdot a \neq P \\ 1 & \text{if } P \cdot a = P \end{cases}$$

  (5) Show that a language L is in $A^*\mathscr{R}$ if and only if it is a union of classes modulo $\equiv_n$ for a certain integer $n > 0$.

Chapter 5

Complementary Results

In this final chapter we present without proof the main results and open problems concerning varieties of languages. Certain statements have been deliberately weakened to avoid too technical conditions. Once again in this chapter, the semigroups are assumed to be finite except in the case of free semigroups.

1. Operations

1.1. Operations on languages

We have already used several operations on languages: boolean operations, quotient, product, star and inverse morphisms. There exist many others which are used to a greater or lesser extent in the theory of languages. We give here some examples, with first of all morphisms between free monoids. Since we are concerned here with a very powerful operation, we often impose on it supplementary conditions. Thus a morphism $\varphi: A^* \to B^*$ is **length preserving** (or 'strictly alphabetic') if, for every $a \in A$, $a\varphi$ is a letter of B. φ is a **coding**, a **prefix coding**, a **suffix coding**, a **biprefix coding**, etc. if φ is injective and if $A\varphi$ is a code of B^*, a prefix code, a suffix code, a biprefix code, etc. respectively. For example the morphism $\varphi: \{a, b, c\}^* \to \{a, b\}^*$ defined by $a\varphi = a$, $b\varphi = ba$ and $c\varphi = b^2$ is a prefix coding.

The **shuffle** of two words u and v of A^* is the language

$$u \sqcup v = \{u_1 v_1 u_2 v_2 \ldots u_n v_n \mid n \geq 0, u_1, \ldots, u_n, v_1, \ldots, v_n \in A^* \quad \text{and} \quad u_1 \ldots u_n = u$$
$$v_1 \ldots v_n = v\}$$

For example $ab \sqcup ba = \{abba, baba, abab, baab\}$. By extension the shuffle of two languages L_1 and L_2 is the language

$$L_1 \sqcup L_2 = \bigcup_{(u_1, u_2) \in L_1 \times L_2} u_1 \sqcup u_2$$

For example $(ab)^* \sqcup (ab)^* = (a(ab)^*b)^*$ (left as an exercise). We can show that shuffle is an associative operation.

A **substitution** $\sigma: A^* \to B^*$ is a relation from A^* into B^* such that $1\sigma = \{1\}$ and such that, for every $u, v \in A^*$, $(uv)\sigma = (u\sigma)(v\sigma)$. In agreement with the definitions of Chapter 0, the **inverse substitution** $\sigma^{-1}: B^* \to A^*$ is defined, for every word $u \in B^*$, by $u\sigma^{-1} = \{v \in A^* \mid u \in v\sigma\}$. If L is a language of B^*, the definition can be extended by putting $L\sigma^{-1} = \{v \in A^* \mid v\sigma \cap L \neq \varnothing\}$.

Example 1.1

Let $\sigma: A^* \to A^*$ be the substitution defined by $a\sigma = \{1, a\}$ for every $a \in A$. Then we can show that, for every language $L \subset A^*$, $L\sigma^{-1} = L \sqcup A^*$.

The concatenation product admits several interesting variants. Let $L_0, L_1, \ldots, L_n \subset A^*$ be languages and $a_1, \ldots, a_n \in A$ be letters and consider the product $L = L_0 a_1 L_1 a_2 \ldots a_n L_n$. For various reasons, this product operation with insertion of letters is more important than the usual concatenation product. For example, Schützenberger's algorithm for star-free expressions (see Chapter 4) always uses products of this type.

We shall say that the product $L = L_0 a_1 L_1 a_2 \ldots a_n L_n$ is **unambiguous** if every word u of L admits a *unique* decomposition of the form $u = u_0 a_1 u_1 a_2 \ldots a_n u_n$ with $u_0 \in L_0, \ldots, u_n \in L_n$. The product is called **deterministic** if for $i = 1, \ldots, n$ the languages $L_0 a_1 L_1 \ldots L_{i-1} a_i$ are prefix codes. The product is **antideterministic** if for every $i = 0, \ldots, n$ the languages $a_i L_i \ldots a_n L_n$ are suffix codes. It is easy to see that every determinstic or antideterministic product is unambiguous. For example, if $A_0, A_1, \ldots, A_n$ are subsets of A such that, for $i = 1, \ldots, n$, $a_i \notin A_{i-1}$, the product $A_0^* a_1 A_1^* a_2 \ldots a_n A_n^*$ is deterministic.

A **sequential function** $\sigma: A^* \to B^*$ is a function from A^* into B^* whose behaviour is described by a machine called a 'sequential transducer'. Formally a **sequential transducer** is a sextuplet $\mathcal{T} = (Q, A, B, q_0, \cdot, *)$ where $(Q, A, \cdot)$ is a finite automaton, q_0 is an element of Q called the initial state and $*$ is an output function, i.e. a function $(q, a) \to q * a$ from $Q \times A$ into B^* which can be extended to a function

$$Q \times A^* \to B^*$$

by putting for $u \in A^*$ and $a \in A$

$$q * 1 = 1$$

$$q * ua = (q * u)((q \cdot u) * a)$$

A function $\sigma: A^* \to B^*$ is called **sequential** if there exists a sequential transducer $\mathcal{T} = (Q, A, B, q_0, \cdot, *)$ such that, for every word $u \in A^*$, $u\sigma = q_0 * u$.

The examples which follow illustrate the importance of sequential functions in the theory of languages. In these examples the sequential transducers are represented by diagrams similar to those used to represent automata. The initial state is indicated by an arrow and we represent the formulae $q \cdot a = q'$ and $q * a = u$ by the diagram

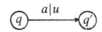

Example 1.2

Let $\sigma: \{a, b\}^* \to \{a, b, c\}^*$ be the sequential function realized by the transducer

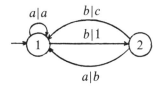

To obtain the image of a word under σ it is sufficient to 'read' this word into the transducer, starting with the initial state and noting the outputs sequentially. For example, if $u = ababb$, the automaton passes successively into the states $1, 1, 2, 1, 2, 1$ and produces successively the outputs $a, 1, b, 1, c$. Hence we deduce that $u\sigma = abc$.

We can observe (as an exercise) that $\sigma^{-1}: \{a, b, c\}^* \to \{a, b\}^*$ is the prefix coding defined by $a\sigma^{-1} = a$, $b\sigma^{-1} = ba$ and $c\sigma^{-1} = bb$. This example is generic. If φ is a prefix coding, φ^{-1} is a sequential function.

Example 1.3

Let $\sigma: a^* \to a^*$ be the sequential function realized by the sequential transducer

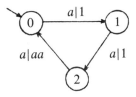

We see that, for every $n \geq 0$, $(a^{3n})\sigma = (a^{3n+1})\sigma = (a^{3n+2})\sigma = a^{2n}$.

Example 1.4

Let $A = \{a, b\}$ and let $\sigma: A^* \to a^*$ be the function defined for every $u \in A^*$ by $u\sigma = a^n$ where n is the number of factors of u equal to aba. This function is realized by the sequential transducer

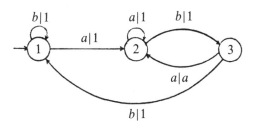

This example is generic; we can count the number of factors of a word equal to a given word with the help of a sequential function.

Example 1.5

Let $A = \{a, b\}$ and $\sigma: A^*abaA^* \to A^*$ be the function which replaces, in a word u, the first occurrence of aba by a. Formally $u\sigma = u$ if aba is not a factor of u and, if $u = u_1abau_2$ and aba is not a factor of u_1ab, then $u\sigma = u_1au_2$. This function is realized by the sequential transducer

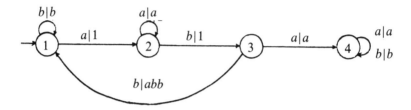

The last three examples are arithmetical operations on the integers. To show the sequential character of these operations, we must code the integers by words of the alphabet $\{0, 1\}$. For this purpose we use a *reverse* binary representation. In other words, the word $a_0a_1 \ldots a_n \in \{0, 1\}^*$ represents the number

$$\sum_{0 \le i \le n} a_i 2^{n-i}$$

We note that the same number admits an infinity of representations. Thus all the words of the form 0110^n represent the number 6. Exceptionally, the empty word will be denoted by ε.

Example 1.6

Let $\sigma: \{0, 1\}^* \to \{0, 1\}^*$ be the sequential function realized by the transducer

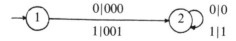

We see that, if u represents n, $u\sigma$ represents $4n$.

Example 1.7

Let $\sigma: \{0, 1\}^* \to \{0, 1\}^*$ be the sequential function realized by the transducer in Fig. 1. The reader will be able to verify that, if $u \in \{0, 1\}^*000$ and if u represents n, $u\sigma$ represents $5n$. For example $(111000)\sigma = 110001$ and $7 \cdot 5 = 35$.

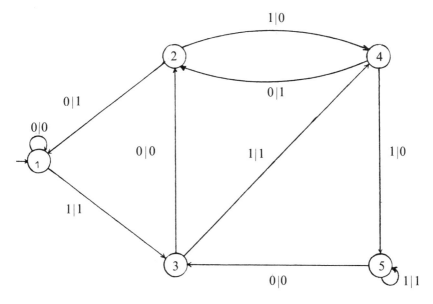

Fig. 1.

Example 1.8

Let $\sigma:\{0,1\}^* \to \{0,1\}^*$ be the sequential function realized by the transducer in Fig. 2. We can verify that, if $u \in \{0,1\}^*00$ and if u codes n, $u\sigma$ codes the integer $n\varphi$ equal to $n/2$ if n is even and equal to $3n+1$ if n is odd. A famous conjecture states that for every integer n the set $\{n\varphi^k \mid k \geqslant 0\}$ is finite ... .

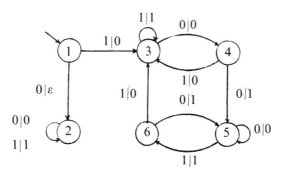

Fig. 2.

1.2. Operations on monoids

Given an operation φ which associates with n languages $L_1, \ldots, L_n$ of A^* a language $L = (L_1, \ldots, L_n)\varphi$ of B^*, the first question which arises is to determine whether φ preserves the property of being recognizable. If this is the case, we can then refine the theory and determine a monoid recognizing L as a function of monoids $M_1, \ldots, M_n$ recognizing $L_1, \ldots, L_n$ respectively. In other words, we seek theorems of the type 'if, for $1 \le i \le n$, M_i recognizes L_i, then the monoid $(M_1, \ldots, M_n)\Phi$ recognizes the language $(L_1, \ldots, L_n)\varphi$'. The problem then reduces to associating with an operation φ on languages an operation Φ on monoids. We observe that this problem was solved in Chapter 1 for boolean operations, quotients and inverse morphisms. There exists in fact a general method for obtaining this type of theorem (see the work of J. Sakarovitch and J. E. Pin). The method can be applied to all the interesting operations with the exception of the star (and the operation 'plus' if we are working in free semigroups). It uses properties of relations between free monoids which are beyond the scope of this chapter but which are expounded in the book *Transductions and Context Free Languages* by J. Berstel (Chapters 3 and 4). Accordingly we shall content ourselves here with mentioning some results. We recall that, if M is a monoid, $\mathscr{P}(M)$ denotes the monoid of subsets of M, together with the following product:

$$\text{if } \quad X, Y \in \mathscr{P}(M) \qquad XY = \{xy \mid x \in X \quad \text{and} \quad y \in Y\}$$

Proposition 1.1

Let $\varphi : A^* \to B^*$ be a literal morphism. If $L \subset A^*$ is recognized by a monoid M, $L\varphi$ is recognized by $\mathscr{P}(M)$.

Proposition 1.2

Let $\sigma : A^* \to B^*$ be a substitution. If $K \subset B^*$ is recognized by a monoid M, $K\sigma^{-1}$ is recognized by $\mathscr{P}(M)$.

Proposition 1.3

If L_1 and L_2 are languages of A^* recognized by M_1 and M_2 respectively, $L_1 \sqcup\!\sqcup L_2$ is recognized by $\mathscr{P}(M_1 \times M_2)$.

The study of the concatenation product leads to the definition of Schützenberger's product of n monoids.

Let M be a monoid. As we have seen $\mathscr{P}(M)$ is a monoid with the intersection of subsets as an operation. It is also a commutative monoid for union. For this reason we shall denote by $P + Q$ the union of two subsets P and Q of M, and for consistency we shall denote by 0 the empty subset and by 1 the subset $\{1\}$. We can verify immediately the following formulae where $P, P_1, P_2 \subset M$:

$$(P_1 + P_2)P = P_1 P + P_2 P \qquad\qquad P(P_1 + P_2) = PP_1 + PP_2$$
$$0P = 0 = P0 \qquad\qquad\qquad 1P = P = P1$$

We can then, for every integer $n > 0$, define the monoid $\mathscr{P}(M)^{n \times n}$ of matrices of size $n \times n$ with entries in $\mathscr{P}(M)$, with the usual matrix product.

Let $M_1, \ldots, M_n$ be monoids and let $M = M_1 \times \ldots \times M_n$. The **Schützenberger product** of $M_1, \ldots, M_n$, denoted by $\Diamond_n(M_1, \ldots, M_n)$, is the submonoid of $\mathscr{P}(M)^{n \times n}$ composed of all the matrices P satisfying the following three conditions:

(1) $P_{ij} = 0$ if $i > j$

(2) $P_{ii} = \{(1,\ldots,1,m_i,1,\ldots,1)\}$ for a certain $m_i \in M_i$

       ↑

    ith component

(3) $P_{ij} \subset \{(m_1,\ldots,m_n) \in M \,|\, m_1 = \ldots = m_{i-1} = 1 = m_{j+1} = \ldots = m_n\}$
for $1 \leq i \leq j \leq n$

Condition (2) enables us to identify the element P_{ii} with an element of M_i. With this convention a matrix of $\Diamond_3(M_1, M_2, M_3)$ will have the form

$$\begin{pmatrix} m_1 & P_{12} & P_{13} \\ 0 & m_2 & P_{23} \\ 0 & 0 & m_3 \end{pmatrix}$$

where $m_i \in M_i$ for $i = 1, 2, 3$ and where P_{12}, P_{13} and P_{23} are subsets of M consisting of elements of the form $(m_1, m_2, 1)$, (m_1, m_2, m_3) and $(1, m_2, m_3)$ respectively.

We note that the Schützenberger product is not associative, in the sense that in general the monoids $\Diamond_2(M_1, \Diamond_2(M_2, M_3))$, $\Diamond_3(M_1, M_2, M_3)$ and $\Diamond_2(\Diamond_2(M_1, M_2), M_3)$ are pairwise distinct.

Finally, we have the following result due to Schützenberger for $n = 1$ and to Straubing in the general case.

Theorem 1.4

Let $L_0, L_1, \ldots, L_n \subset A^*$ be languages recognized by monoids $M_0, \ldots, M_n$ and $a_1, a_2, \ldots, a_n$ be letters of A. Then the languages $L_0 L_1 \ldots L_n$ and $L_0 a_1 L_1 a_2 \ldots a_n L_n$ are recognized by the monoid $\Diamond_{n+1}(M_0, \ldots, M_n)$.

This theorem admits a partial converse due to Reutenauer for $n = 1$ and to Pin in the general case.

Theorem 1.5

If $L \subset A^*$ is recognized by $\Diamond_{n+1}(M_0, \ldots, M_n)$, then L is in the boolean algebra generated by languages of the form $L_{i_0} a_1 L_{i_1} a_2 \ldots a_r L_{i_r}$ where $0 \leq i_0 < i_1 \ldots < i_r \leq r$, and, for $1 \leq k \leq r$, $a_k \in A$ and L_{i_k} is a language recognized by M_{i_k}.

Finally sequential functions are related to two very important operations on semigroups: the semidirect product and the wreath product.

Let S and T be two semigroups. To simplify the notation we shall represent S additively (without necessarily supposing that S is commutative) and T multiplicatively. In particular, if S and T are monoids, we shall denote by 0 and 1 the identities of S and T respectively.

A (left) **action** of T and S is a function

$$T \times S \to S$$

$$(t, s) \to t \cdot s$$

satisfying for every $t, t_1, t_2 \in T$ and $s, s_1, s_2 \in S$

$$t \cdot (s_1 + s_2) = t \cdot s_1 + t \cdot s_2 \tag{1}$$

$$t_1 \cdot (t_2 \cdot s) = (t_1 t_2) \cdot s \tag{2}$$

If S is a monoid, we say that the action is **right unitary** if

$$t \cdot 0 = 0 \text{ for every } t \in T \tag{3}$$

If T is a monoid, we say that the action is **left unitary** if

$$1 \cdot s = s \text{ for every } s \in S \tag{4}$$

An action is **unitary** if it is simultaneously right and left unitary.

Given an action of T on S, the **semidirect product** $S * T$ is the semigroup defined on $S \times T$ by the multiplication

$$(s, t)(s', t') = (s + t \cdot s', tt')$$

If S and T are monoids and if the action of T on S is unitary, $S * T$ is a monoid with identity $(0, 1)$.

The **wreath product** $S \circ T$ of S and T is the semidirect product $S^{T^1} * T$ defined by the action of T on S^{T^1} given by the following formula, where $f : T^1 \to S$ is a function and where $t \in T$:

$$t \cdot f : T^1 \to S \text{ is the function defined by } t'(t \cdot f) = (t't)f$$

Consequently the multiplication in $S \circ T$ is given by the formula $(f_1, t_1)(f_2, t_2) = (f, t_1 t_2)$ where, for all $t \in T^1$, $tf = tf_1 + (tt_1)f_2$. The wreath product is in a way the most general semidirect product. We can show in fact that, for every left action of T on S, $S * T$ is a subsemigroup of $S \circ T$.

The link with sequential functions is simple.

Theorem 1.6

Let $\sigma : A^* \to B^*$ be a sequential function realized by a transducer $\mathcal{T} = (Q, A, B, q_0, \cdot, *)$ and let $M(\sigma)$ be the transition monoid of the automaton $(Q, A, \cdot)$. If $L \subset B^*$ is recognized by a monoid M, then $L\sigma^{-1}$ is recognized by $M \circ M(\sigma)$.

This general theorem has very numerous applications in view of the diversity of sequential functions. It admits a partial converse which has been used in particular cases by various workers. The version below is due to H. Straubing.

Let M and N be two monoids and let $\eta : A^* \to M \circ N$ be a morphism. We denote by $\pi : M \circ N \to N$ the morphism defined by $(f, n)\pi = n$ and we put $\varphi = \eta\pi$. φ is then a morphism from A^* into N. Let $B = N \times A$ and $\sigma : A^* \to B^*$ be the sequential function defined by

$$(a_1 \ldots a_n)\sigma = (1, a_1)(a_1\varphi, a_2) \ldots ((a_1 \ldots a_{n-1}\varphi), a_n)$$

We note that σ is realized by the transducer $\mathscr{T} = (N, A, B, \cdot, *)$ whose transitions are given by the diagram

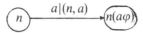

where $n \in N$ and $a \in A$.

This being the case, we can state the 'wreath product principle'.

Theorem 1.7

If a language L is recognized by $\eta: A^* \to M \circ N$, then L is a finite boolean combination of languages of the form $X \cap Y\sigma^{-1}$ where $Y \subset B^*$ is recognized by M and where $X \subset A^*$ is recognized by N.

1.3. Operations on varieties

In general, if $\varphi: A^* \times \ldots \times A^* \to B^*$ is an n-ary operation, we shall say that a $*$-variety of language $\mathscr{V}$ is closed under the operation φ if $L_1, \ldots, L_n \in A^*\mathscr{V}$ implies $(L_1, \ldots, L_n)\varphi \in B^*\mathscr{V}$. We have of course an analogous definition for $+$-varieties of languages. For example every variety is closed, by definition, under boolean operations and inverse morphisms. The statements which follow provide other examples.

Theorem 1.8 (Perrot)

The only $*$-variety closed under star is the variety of rational languages.

Theorem 1.9 (Pin)

The only $+$-varieties closed under the operation $L \to L^+$ are the trivial variety, the variety of rational languages and the varieties of languages $\mathscr{K}_1$ and $\mathscr{K}_1^t$.

A little further on we shall study various restrictions of the operations star and plus. The problem of characterization of varieties closed under shuffle remains open.

Problem 1.1

Prove or disprove the following conjecture: the only $*$-variety closed under shuffle is the variety of rational languages.

We have nevertheless a partial result (for more details see the article '*Variétés de langages et monoïdes des parties*' by J. E. Pin).

Theorem 1.10

Every $*$-variety closed under shuffle contains the variety $\mathscr{J}$ of piecewise-testable languages and the variety $\mathscr{C}$om of commutative languages.

In contrast, we have more precise results for morphisms.

Theorem 1.11
The only variety closed under morphisms is the variety of rational languages.

This statement is as true for $+$-varieties as for $*$-varieties and can even be strengthened.

Theorem 1.12
The only variety closed under coding is the variety of rational languages.

If V is a variety of monoids, we denote by PV the variety of monoids generated by the monoids $\mathscr{P}(M)$ for $M \in V$. By extension, we put $P^0 V = V$ and for $n \geq 0$ $P^{n+1} V = P(P^n V)$. We then have the following result, which is an amalgam of the works of Reutenauer, Straubing and Pin.

Theorem 1.13
Let V be a variety of monoids and $\mathscr{V}$ and $\mathscr{W}$ be the varieties of languages corresponding respectively to V and PV. Then for every alphabet A

(1) $A^*\mathscr{W}$ is the boolean algebra generated by the languages of the form $L\varphi$ where $L \in B^*\mathscr{V}$ and where $\varphi : B^* \to A^*$ is a length-preserving morphism
(2) $A^*\mathscr{W}$ is the boolean algebra generated by the languages of the form $L\sigma^{-1}$ where $L \in B^*\mathscr{V}$ and where $\sigma : A^* \to B^*$ is a substitution

We can summarize this result schematically by saying that the operator P corresponds to length-preserving morphisms or to inverses of substitutions. This theorem explains the importance of the study of monoids of the form $\mathscr{P}(M)$ and of varieties of the form PV. At present the classification of varieties of this type has not been achieved. However, the following is a list of results obtained by Margolis, Perrot, Putcha, Straubing and Pin in particular.

Theorem 1.14
If V is the trivial variety, $PV = J_1$ is the variety of idempotent and commutative monoids, $P^2 V$ is the variety of aperiodic and commutative monoids and $P^3 V = P^2 V$.

Theorem 1.15
If V is a non-trivial variety contained in **Com**, PV is the variety of commutative monoids whose groups are elements of V and $P^2 V = PV$.

Theorem 1.16
(1) If V contains a non-commutative monoid, then $P^3 V = M$.
(2) If V contains a non-commutative group, then $P^2 V = M$.

Let R_1 be the variety of idempotent and $\mathscr{R}$-trivial monoids.

Theorem 1.17
The varieties R_1, PR_1, P^2R_1 and $P^3R_1 = M$ are distinct.

We denote by DS and DA the variety of monoids whose regular $\mathscr{D}$-classes are semigroups and aperiodic semigroups respectively. Let BA_2 be the semigroup of matrices

$$\left\{ \begin{pmatrix} 1 & 0 \\ 0 & 0 \end{pmatrix}, \begin{pmatrix} 0 & 1 \\ 0 & 0 \end{pmatrix}, \begin{pmatrix} 0 & 0 \\ 1 & 0 \end{pmatrix}, \begin{pmatrix} 0 & 0 \\ 0 & 1 \end{pmatrix}, \begin{pmatrix} 0 & 0 \\ 0 & 0 \end{pmatrix} \right\}$$

with standard matrix multiplication.

Theorem 1.18
Let V be a variety of monoids. The following conditions are equivalent:

(1) $PV = M$
(2) the monoid $BA_2{}^1$ is an element of M
(3) V is not contained in DS

Theorem 1.19
The following equalities hold: $PJ = PR = PR^r = PDA$.

We can also characterize the varieties V such that $PV \subset J$, $PV \subset R$, $PV \subset R^r$ and $PV \subset A \ldots$. Further results concerning the varieties PV when V is a variety of semigroups have been obtained by Almeida. In particular Almeida has obtained a description of all the varieties of semigroups V such that $PV = V$ but the situation is much more involved than in the case of varieties of monoids. We give in conclusion three open problems.

Problem 1.2
Determine the varieties V such that $P^2V = M$.

A variety of monoids V is called **decidable** if there exists an algorithm to test whether a given monoid belongs to V. The monoid M under test is given for example by its multiplication table and the algorithm must produce 1 if $M \in V$ and 0 otherwise.

Problem 1.3
Is the variety PJ decidable?

The same question can be posed for other varieties. In particular the following can be posed.

Problem 1.4
Are the varieties PG and PDS decidable?

The characterization of varieties closed under product is one of the most important results of recent years. It alone justifies the introduction of relational morphisms.

Theorem 1.20 (Straubing)

A $*$-variety of languages $\mathscr{V}$ is closed under product if and only if the corresponding variety of monoids V satisfies $A^{-1}V = V$.

In particular the variety of star-free languages is the smallest variety closed under product. Straubing's original proof uses the properties of the wreath product. A proof by induction, in the spirit of the proof of Schützenberger's theorem (Chapter 4) has been given by Pin, and a third proof using categories instead of monoids has recently been proposed by Pin, Straubing and Thérien. These last two proofs also provide a characterization of varieties closed under unambiguous product, deterministic product, or antideterministic product. We specify that a $*$-class $\mathscr{C}$ is closed under unambiguous product, deterministic product or antideterministic product if, for every alphabet A, $A^*\mathscr{C}$ contains every unambiguous (deterministic, antideterministic) product of the form $L_0 a_1 L_1 a_2 \dots a_n L_n$ where $L_0, \dots, L_n \in A^*\mathscr{C}$ and $a_1, \dots, a_n \in A$.

Theorem 1.21

Let $\mathscr{V}$ be a variety of languages and let V be the corresponding variety of monoids. Then $\mathscr{V}$ is closed under unambiguous product, deterministic product or antideterministic product if and only if $V = LI^{-1}V$, $V = K^{-1}V$ and $V = (K^{\tau})^{-1}V$ respectively.

The same method enables us to state Chapter 4, Theorem 3.3, more precisely and to describe the variety of languages $\mathscr{D}\mathscr{A}$ corresponding to DA.

Theorem 1.22

For every alphabet A, $A^*\mathscr{R}$ or $A^*\mathscr{R}'$ is the smallest class of languages of A^* containing languages of the form B^*, with $B \subset A$, and closed under disjoint union and deterministic product or antideterministic product respectively.

Theorem 1.23 (Schützenberger)

For every alphabet A, $A^*\mathscr{D}\mathscr{A}$ is the smallest class of languages of A^* containing languages of the form B^*, with $B \subset A$, and closed under disjoint union and unambiguous product.

We observe that, since $Nil \subset DA$, se must find the finite languages in $\mathscr{D}\mathscr{A}$. Indeed if L is a finite language we have

$$L = \bigcup_{u \in L} \{u\}$$

the union being disjoint, and, if $u = a_1 \dots a_n$

$$\{u\} = \varnothing^* a_1 \varnothing^* a_2 \dots a_n \varnothing^*$$

this product being unambiguous.

We can also make use of the ambiguity of the concatenation product to describe other varieties of languages. Let L_1, L_2 be languages of A^*, a be a letter of A and r, n be two positive integers. We put $(L_1 a L_2)_{r,n} = \{u \in A^* \mid$ the number of factorizations of the type $u = u_1 a u_2$ with $u_1 \in L_1$ and $u_2 \in L_2$ is congruent to r modulo $n\}$.

Let Gsol be the variety of solvable groups and let $\mathscr{G}$sol be the corresponding variety of languages. We then have the following statements, which follow from the works of Straubing and Thérien.

Theorem 1.24
For every alphabet A, $A^*\mathscr{G}$sol is the smallest boolean algebra $\mathscr{C}$ such that, if $a \in A, 0 \le r < n$ and $L_1, L_2 \in \mathscr{C}$, then $(L_1 a L_2)_{r,n} \in A^*\mathscr{C}$.

Likewise we denote by $\bar{G}$sol the variety of monoids all of whose groups are solvable and by $\bar{\mathscr{G}}$sol the corresponding variety of languages.

Theorem 1.25
For every alphabet A, $A^*\bar{\mathscr{G}}$sol is the smallest boolean algebra $\mathscr{C}$ such that, if $a \in A, 0 \le r < n$ and $L_1, L_2 \in \mathscr{C}$, then

(a) $L_1 a L_2 \in \mathscr{C}$
(b) $(L_1 a L_2)_{r,n} \in \mathscr{C}$

If V and W are two varieties of semigroups, we denote by $V * W$ the variety of semigroups generated by all the semidirect products of the form $S * T$ with $S \in V$ and $T \in W$. In the same way, if V and W are two varieties of monoids, we denote by $V * W$ the variety of monoids generated by all the semidirect products of the form $S * T$ with $S \in V$ and $T \in W$ and such that the action of T on S is unitary. Finally if V is a variety of monoids and W is a variety of semigroups, or if V is a variety of monoids, we denote by $V * W$ the variety of semigroups generated by the semidirect products $S * T$ with $S \in V$ and $T \in W$ and such that the action of T on S is right unitary or left unitary respectively. We have in all cases the following.

Theorem 1.26 (Eilenberg)
The operation $*$ defined on varieties is associative.

The study of varieties of the form $V * W$ is closely related to the study of sequential functions and of the wreath product (see Theorem 1.6 and 1.7). The following are some examples of results obtained by these techniques. In these statements V denotes a variety of monoids and $\mathscr{V}$ is the corresponding $*$-variety of languages.

Theorem 1.27
Let $\mathscr{W}$ be the $*$-variety of languages corresponding to $J_1 * V$. Then for every alphabet A, $A^*\mathscr{W}$ is the boolean algebra generated by languages of the form L where LaA^* with $a \in A$ and $L \in A^*\mathscr{V}$.

Theorem 1.28

Let $\mathcal{W}$ be the variety of languages corresponding to $R * V$. Then for every alphabet A, $A^*\mathcal{W}$ is the smallest boolean algebra containing $A * \mathcal{V}$ and closed under the operations $L \to LaA^*$ where $a \in A$.

Theorem 1.29 (Straubing)

Let $\mathcal{W}$ be the variety of languages corresponding to $G\text{com} * V$. Then for every alphabet A, $A^*\mathcal{W}$ is the smallest boolean algebra $\mathcal{C}$ containing $A^*\mathcal{V}$ and such that, for every $0 < r < n$, $a \in A$ and $L \in A^*\mathcal{V}$, $(LaA^*)_{r,n} \in \mathcal{C}$.

Straubing has recently proved a similar result for the operation $V \to V * LI$. We shall see other examples in Section 3. There remain many problems to be solved on varieties of the type $V * W$. The most important of these is the following.

Problem 1.5

If V and W are decidable varieties, is $V * W$ decidable?

A particular case of this problem is well known in the theory of semigroups. Put $W_0 = A$ and, for $n \geq 0$, $W_{n+1} = W_n * G * A$. We then have the following theorem.

Theorem 1.30 (Krohn–Rhodes)

$$\bigcup_{n \geq 0} W_n = M$$

Now, given a monoid M, the problem is to determine its complexity, i.e. the smallest integer n such that $M \in W_n$. This reduces to determining whether the varieties W_n are decidable. It is clear that W_0 is decidable and Karnofsky and Rhodes have established the decidability of the varieties $A * G$ and $G * A$. However, the problem remains open for the variety $W_1 = A * G * A \dots$.

The second type of problem is the algebraic study of the operation $V * W$. We give some important relations:

$V * V = V$ if $V = I, G, A, R, R * G, G\text{sol}$ for the varieties of monoids
and $V = T, Nil, K, K^{\mathrm{r}}, LI, (A)_S, (R)_S * G, LR, L(R * G), LG$ and, for
every $n \geq 1$, Nil_n and K_n for the varieties of semigroups

We note, however, that this equality is no longer true for $V = (G)_S$ and $V = K^{\mathrm{r}}_n$ for $n \geq 1$:

$V * LI = LV$ if $V = J_1, R, R * G$ or if V is a variety of groups
$V * LI = V * K^{\mathrm{r}}$ for every non-trivial variety of monoids (Straubing)
$K^{\mathrm{r}} * V \subset V * K^{\mathrm{r}}$ for every variety of monoids (Stiffler)
$G * R \subset R * G$ (Stiffler)

The third type of problem is to determine the equations of varieties of the form $V * W$. This problem seems to be difficult even for the simplest varieties. For example, Pin has proved that the variety $J_1 * J_1$ is defined by the equations $(xuyv)xy = (xuyv)yx$ and $xux = xux^2$ but we do not know even whether the varieties $J_1 * (\mathbb{Z}_2)$ and $J_1 * J_1 * J_1$ are defined by a finite number of equations. However, Ash has shown that the variety $J_1 * G = Inv$ (see Chapter 3, Problems 1.8 and 1.9) is defined by the equation $x^\omega y^\omega = y^\omega x^\omega$.

2. Concatenation hierarchies

2.1. Locally testable languages

Let $L \subset A^+$ be a recognizable language and u a word of A^+. If the set of factors of length less than or equal to n of a word u determines whether it belongs to L, L is called locally n-testable. Here is a more precise definition. For every $n > 0$ consider the congruence $\sim_n$ over A^+ defined by $u \sim_n v$ if and only if the following hold.

(a) u and v have the same left factors of length less than n.
(b) u and v have the same right factors of length less than n.
(c)   The set of factors of length n of u is equal to the set of factors of length n of v.

For example $abaabaaba \sim_3 abaaba$. A language is called **locally n-testable** if it is the union of $\sim_n$-classes. A language is called *locally testable* if it is locally n-testable for a certain integer $n > 0$.

Locally testable languages have been characterized independently by Brzozowski and Simon and by McNaughton.

Theorem 2.1

Let L be a recognizable language of A^+. The following conditions are equivalent.

(1) L is locally testable.
(2) L is in the boolean algebra generated by the languages of the form uA^*, A^*v or A^*wA^* where $u, v, w \in A^+$.
(3)   The syntactic semigroup S of L is locally idempotent and commutative, i.e. for every $e \in E(S)$, eSe is idempotent and commutative.

Thus, if $A = \{a, b\}$, the language $L = (ab)^+$ is locally testable since $(ab)^+ = (aA^* \cap A^*b) \backslash (A^*aaA^* \cup A^*bbA^*)$. We can also verify directly that $S(L)$ is locally idempotent and commutative. Theorem 2.1 shows that locally testable languages form a variety of languages denoted by $\mathscr{L}t$. We recall that we denote by LJ_1 the variety of locally idempotent and commutative semigroups. We have then the following theorem.

Theorem 2.2

The variety of semigroups corresponding to $\mathscr{L}t$ is $LJ_1 = J_1 * LI$.
It is quite easy to establish directly that $J_1 * LI$ is the variety of semigroups which corresponds to $\mathscr{L}t$. The equality $LJ_1 = J_1 * LI$ is much more difficult to

establish and constitutes a key theorem of the theory. It was one of the starting points that led to the general study of the operation $V * LI$(Straubing, Tilson).

2.2.   General results on concatenation hierarchies

Let A be a finite alphabet. The following is a general procedure for constructing a concatenation hierarchy. We are given at the outset a boolean algebra $\mathscr{F}_0$ of languages of A^* or A^+ which will constitute level 0 of the hierarchy. To pass from level n to level $n + 1$, we define $\mathscr{F}_{n+1}$ as the boolean algebra generated by the languages of the form $L_0 a_1 L_1 a_2 \ldots a_k L_k$ where $k \geq 0$, $L_0, \ldots, L_k \in \mathscr{F}_n$ and $a_1, \ldots, a_k \in A$. We thus obtain an ascending hierarchy (not necessarily strict) $\mathscr{F}_0 \subset \mathscr{F}_1 \subset \ldots \subset \mathscr{F}_n \subset \ldots$.

If now $\mathscr{V}_0$ is a *-variety (or +-variety) of languages, we can consider, for each alphabet A, the hierarchy whose initial point is $A^*\mathscr{V}_0$ (or $A^+\mathscr{V}_0$ respectively): $A^*\mathscr{V}_1, \ldots, A^*\mathscr{V}_n, \ldots$ (or $A^+\mathscr{V}_0, A^+\mathscr{V}_1, \ldots, A^+\mathscr{V}_n, \ldots$). We then have the following theorem.

Theorem 2.3
For every $n \geq 0$, $\mathscr{V}_n$ is a variety of languages.

Although there are certainly other interesting cases, three cases only have been considered in the literature. Cohen and Brzozowski introduced the 'dot-depth hierarchy' in 1971 and Straubing defined another hierarchy in 1982. The third example was considered by Margolis and Pin in 1985. However, we shall not follow the historical order for our presentation.

Each level of a hierarchy contains a subhierarchy that can be defined in the following way. For every $m \geq 0$, we define $\mathscr{F}_{n+1,m}$ as the boolean algebra generated by the languages of the form $L_0 a_1 L_1 \ldots a_k L_k$ where $0 \leq k \leq m$, $L_0, \ldots, L_k \in \mathscr{F}_n$ and $a_1, \ldots, a_k \in A$. We have then

$$\mathscr{F}_{n+1} = \bigcup_{m > 0} \mathscr{F}_{n+1,m}$$

As before, if we start from a variety of languages $\mathscr{V}_0$, we are led to varieties of languages $\mathscr{V}_{n,m}$ for every $n, m \geq 0$.

We can in fact construct hierarchies of still more complex varieties, indexed no longer by integers but by trees (see Pin, 'Hierarchies de concaténation' for a discussion).

2.3.   Straubing's hierarchy

This hierarchy is obtained by starting from the trivial *-variety of languages. We have then, for every alphabet A, $A^*\mathscr{V}_0 = \{\varnothing, A^*\}$. We shall denote by V_n the variety of monoids corresponding to $\mathscr{V}_n$. In particular $V_0 = I$. It follows immediately from the definition that $A^*\mathscr{V}_1$ is the boolean algebra generated by the languages of the form $A^* a_1 A^* a_2 \ldots a_k A^*$ with $k \geq 0$ and $a_1, \ldots, a_k \in A$. Consequently $\mathscr{V}_1$ is the variety of piecewise-testable languages and, from Simon's theorem, $V_1 = J$. We then have an algorithm to test whether a recognizable language is of height 1 in Straubing's hierarchy. Level 2 of the hierarchy is described by the following theorem, which is due to Straubing and Pin.

Theorem 2.4
Let L be a language of A^*. The following conditions are equivalent.

(1) $L \in A^* \mathscr{V}_2$.
(2) L is in the boolean algebra generated by the languages of the form $A_0^* a_1 A_1^* a_2 \ldots a_k A_k^*$ where $k \geq 0$, $A_i \subset A$ for $0 \leq i \leq k$ and $a_i \in A$ for $1 \leq i \leq k$.
(3) The syntactic monoid of L is an element of $\boldsymbol{PJ}$.

In other words $V_2 = \boldsymbol{PJ}$, which explains the importance of Problem 1.3; its solution will provide an algorithm to decide whether a recognizable language is of height 2 in Straubing's hierarchy. Straubing (1986) has recently proved the existence of such an algorithm in the case of an alphabet containing at most two letters. We can deduce from Theorem 2.4 a representation theorem for the monoids of $\boldsymbol{PJ}$ which we will be able to compare with Chapter 4, Theorem 1.10. Let T_n be the monoid of boolean (upper) triangular matrices of size $n \times n$.

Theorem 2.5
A monoid is an element of $\boldsymbol{PJ}$ if and only if it divides T_n for a certain integer $n > 0$.

・ Let V be a variety of languages. For every $n > 0$, we denote by $\Diamond_n(V)$ the variety generated by the monoids $\Diamond_n(M_1, \ldots, M_n)$ such that $M_1, \ldots, M_n \in V$ and we put

$$\Diamond V = \bigcup_{n>0} \Diamond_n(V)$$

Using Theorem 1.5, we then have the following.

Theorem 2.6
For every integer $n \geq 0$, $V_{n+1} = \Diamond V_n$. In particular $V_1 = J = \Diamond I$ and $V_2 = \boldsymbol{PJ} = \Diamond J = \Diamond J_1 = \Diamond R = \Diamond R^r = \Diamond DA$.

We do not have precise results on the varieties V_n for $n \geq 3$, except for the following general result which is a consequence of Theorem 2.11 which will be given later.

Theorem 2.7
Straubing's hierarchy is strict; for every $n \geq 0$, V_n is strictly contained in V_{n+1}. Moreover

$$A = \bigcup_{n \geq 0} V_n$$

We have very little information about the subhierarchies $V_{n,m}$, except for $n = 1$.

We denote by J_n the variety generated by the monoid T_{n+1}. This notation is consistent with the notation J_1 introduced in Chapter 1 since T_2 is isomorphic to U_1 and U_1 generates the variety of idempotent and commutative monoids.

Theorem 2.8

For every $n > 0$, we have $J_n = V_{1,n} = \Diamond_{n+1}(I)$. Moreover these varieties are decidable.

Theorem 2.9 (Simon)

The variety J_1 is defined by the equations $xy = yx$ and $x = x^2$. The variety J_2 is defined by the equations $(xy)^2 = (yx)^2$ and $xyxzx = xyzx$.

This result leads naturally to the following question.

Problem 2.1

Can the varieties J_n be defined by a finite number of equations?

2.4. Brzozowski's hierarchy

In fact the hierarchy which we are about to present is slightly different from Brzozowski's original hierarchy. However, this modification concerns only level 0.

The hierarchy is obtained by starting from the $+$-variety of Languages $\mathscr{L}I$. We denote by $\mathscr{B}_n$ the $+$-variety of level n and by B_n the corresponding variety of semigroups. We have then $B_0 = LI$ and, for every alphabet A, $A^+\mathscr{B}_0 = \{XA^*Y \cup Z \mid X, Y, Z$ are finite languages of $A^+\}$. Knast has obtained a characterization of the variety $\mathscr{B}_1$.

Theorem 2.10 (Knast)

Let L be a recognizable language of A^+. The following conditions are equivalent.

(1) $L \in A^+\mathscr{B}_1$.
(2) L is in the boolean algebra generated by the languages of the form $u_0 A^* u_1 A^* \ldots u_{k-1} A^* u_k$ where $k \geq 0$ and $u_1, \ldots, u_k \in A^+$.
(3) The syntactic semigroup S of L satisfies the condition (K):
for every $e_1, e_2 \in E(S)$ and for every $x, y, u, v \in S$, we have $(e_1 x e_2 y)^n e_1 x e_2 v e_1 (u e_2 v e_1)^n = (e_1 x e_2 y)^n e_1 (u e_2 v e_1)^n$ where $n = \text{card}(S)$.

The condition (K) gives an algorithm for testing if a language is of height 1 in Brzozowski's hierarchy. We add that this rather complicated condition arises from a much more natural condition in terms of graph congruences and categories, but we cannot develop this aspect without going beyond the scope of this chapter. We do not have results on the varieties B_n for $n \geq 2$ except for the following result.

Theorem 2.11 (Brzozowski and Knast)
Brzozowski's hierarchy is strict; for every $n \geq 0$, B_n is contained strictly in B_{n+1}. Moreover

$$\bigcup_{n \geq 0} B_n = A$$

Another proof of Theorem 2.11 has been given by Straubing. Little is known about the subhierarchy $\mathscr{B}_{1,m}$, which was called 'dot-depth one hierarchy' by Brzozowski. For every alphabet A, $A^+ \mathscr{B}_{1,m}$ is the boolean algebra generated by the languages of the form $u_0 A^* u_1 A^* \ldots u_{k-1} A^* u_k$ where $0 \leq k \leq m+1$ and $u_0, \ldots, u_k \in A^+$. It is quite easy to see that $\mathscr{B}_{1,1}$ is the variety of locally testable languages described in Section 2.1. Beyond that, we cannot characterize these varieities.

2.5. Connection between the hierarchies of Straubing and Brzozowski

There exist remarkable algebraic relations between the varieties V_n and B_n.

Theorem 2.12 (Straubing)
For every $n \geq 0$, we have $B_n = V_n * LI$ and $V_n = B_n \cap M$.

The second relation signifies that a *monoid* is in B_n if and only if it is in V_n. The first relation implies in particular the relations $B_0 = LI$, $B_1 = J * LI$ and $B_2 = PJ * LI$. This result enables us to obtain the following theorem.

Theorem 2.13 (Margolis–Straubing)
For every $n \geq 0$, the variety B_n is decidable if and only if the variety V_n is decidable.

This result shows in particular that the variety B_2 is decidable if and only if PJ is decidable, which leads us once more to Problem 1.3.

2.6. The group-languages hierarchy

The hierarchy is obtained by starting from the $*$-variety $\mathscr{G}$, corresponding to G, the variety of groups. (Other hierarchies can be obtained, for instance, by considering the varieties of all the p-groups, for some prime number p.) We denote by W_n ($W_{n,m}$) the corresponding hierarchy (subhierarchy) of varieties of monoids. The following theorem summarizes the general results known on this hierarchy.

Theorem 2.14 (Margolis–Pin)
(a) $W_0 = G$ and, for every $n \geq 0$, $W_{n+1} = \Diamond W_n$
(b) For every $n \geq 0$, $W_n \subsetneq W_{n+1}$

(c) $\bigcup_{n \geq 0} W_n = A * G$, and this variety is decidable

These results may be compared with Theorems 2.7 and 2.11. However, contrary to the previous hierarchies, it is not yet known whether the level 1 is a decidable variety. Denote by BG the variety of all monoids M such that, for every idempotent $e, f \in M$, $efe = e$ implies $e = f$. It can be shown that a monoid M is in BG if and only if the submonoid of M generated by all the idempotents of M belongs to J, or if and only if every regular $\mathscr{D}$-class of M is a Brandt semigroup. Then we have the following.

Theorem 2.15 (Margolis–Pin)
The following relations hold:

$$W_1 = \diamondsuit G = PG = J * G \subset J^{-1}G = BG$$

However, we still do not know whether $J * G = J^{-1}G$. If this equality holds, this would show that W_1 (and PG, see Problem 1.4) are decidable. Thus the situation is even more complex than for the two other hierarchies, and there are of course no results at all for the levels greater than or equal to 2. The languages of level 1 also arise in the study of the finite group topology for the free monoid (Reutenauer, Pin).

The only complete result concerns the variety $W_{1,1}$. First, we have the following.

Theorem 2.16 (Margolis–Pin)
The following equalities hold:

$$W_{1,1} = \diamondsuit_2 G = Inv = J_1 * G = J_1^{-1}G$$

and the decidability follows from the deep result of Ash.

Theorem 2.17 (Ash)
The variety Inv is decidable. A monoid M belongs to Inv if and only if, for every idempotent $e, f \in M$, $ef = fe$.

2.7. Hierarchies and symbolic logic

Consider the language $L = A^*aA^*$ over the alphabet $A = \{a, b\}$. The language L is the set of words of A^+ of which one letter is an a. In terms of logic, we shall say that L is the set of words u which satisfy the formula $\exists x R_a x$. Intuitively this formula can be expressed as 'there exists an occurrence of the word which is an a'. Likewise the formula $\varphi = \exists x (R_a x \wedge \forall y (y < x \rightarrow R_b y))$ can be expressed as 'there exists an occurrence of the word which is an a and such that every occurrence which precedes it is a b'. The set of words which satisfy φ is thus the language b^*aA^*.

It remains to formalize what has been said. We shall assume that the basic vocabulary of the logic is known. Let A be a finite alphabet. Consider the set of symbols $\mathscr{L} = \{<\} \cup \{R_a \mid a \in A\}$. In the classical manner, we construct $\mathscr{L}$-

formulae starting from the symbols of $\mathscr{L}$ and logical symbols (equality, logical connections $\vee$, $\wedge$, $\rceil$, $\rightarrow$, variables, the quantifiers $\exists$, $\forall$ and the constants true and false). With each word u of A^+ we associate an $\mathscr{L}$-structure $\mathscr{M}(u)$ $= (M, <, (R_a)_{a \in A})$ where $M = \{1, \ldots, |u|\}$, $<$ is the natural ordering on the integers and, for $a \in A$, R_a is the subset of M defined by $R_a x$ if and only if the xth letter of u is an a. For some technical reasons, we shall not consider the empty word, which would define an empty $\mathscr{L}$-structure. We say that a language L of A^+ **is defined by a statement** φ if L is the set words u of A^+ such that $\mathscr{M}(u)$ is a model for φ. We then have the following results.

Theorem 2.18 (Büchi–Elgot)
A language L of A^+ is recognizable if and only if it can be defined by a monadic weak $\mathscr{L}$-statement of the second order.

Theorem 2.19 (Ladner–McNaughton)
A language L of A^+ is star free if and only if it can be defined by an $\mathscr{L}$-statement of the first order.

W. Thomas has given a much more precise version of this theorem. For this we introduce the set of symbols $\mathscr{L}' = \mathscr{L} \cup \{\min, \max, S, P\}$ and we associate with each word u and $\mathscr{L}'$-structure $\mathscr{M}'(u) = (M, <, \min, \max, S, P, (R_a)_{a \in A}$ where min $= 1$, max $= |u|$, and S and P are successor and predecessor functions. It will be convenient to put $S(\max) = \max$ and $P(\min) = \min$. We define $\mathscr{L}'$-formulae as before. Moreover, we know that every formula of the first order is equivalent to a formula in the normal prefix form, i.e. of the form $\psi = Q(x_1, \ldots, x_k)\varphi$ where $Q(x_1, \ldots, x_k)$ is a sequence of quantifiers $\exists x_i$ or $\forall x_i$ and where φ is a formula without a quantifier. If $Q(x_1, \ldots, x_k)$ is formed of n blocks of quantifiers such that the first block contains only existential quantifiers, the second block only universal quantifiers, etc., we say that ψ is a Σ_n-formula. We denote by Σ_n the set of Σ_n-formulae and by $B\Sigma_n$ the set of boolean combinations of Σ_n-formulae. We have then the following link with Brzozowski's hierarchy.

Theorem 2.20 (Thomas)
A language L of A^+ is an element of $A^+ \mathscr{B}_n$ if and only if it can be defined by an $\mathscr{L}'$-statement of $B\Sigma_n$.

We can in fact adapt Thomas's proof to obtain a similar result for Straubing's hierarchy.

Theorem 2.21
A language L of A^+ is an element of $A^* \mathscr{V}_n$ if and only if it can be defined by an $\mathscr{L}$-statement of $B\Sigma_n$.

Finally W. Thomas has given a purely logical proof of Theorem 2.11.

3. Relations with the theory of codes

The theories of codes and varieties are closely related. The theory of codes was created by Schützenberger in 1956, i.e. at the same time as Kleene's theorem which was the origin of the theory of varieties of languages. The two theories were developed in parallel, and although several results of the theory of codes obtained in the 1960s use syntactic semigroups of the first real link between the two theories was discovered in 1973 by Restivo who gave a very simple characterization of finite codes C such that C^* is star free. Other results followed: we can cite the work of Almeida, De Luca, Eilenberg, T. Hall, Hashigushi-Honda, Keenan, Lallement, E. Le Rest, M. Le Rest, Margolis, Milito, Perrin, Perrot, Pin, Restivo, Reutenauer, Schützenberger, Straubing, Termini, etc. Of course it is impossible to discuss all these results in detail and we have kept here only the results which complement the theorems of the preceding sections. For certain statements, e.g. Theorem 3.2, only the proof is related to the theory of codes.

3.1. Restriction of the operations star and plus

Let X^* be a submonoid of A^*. We say that X^* is **pure** if, for every $n > 0, u^n \in X^*$ implies $u \in X^*$. The operation $X \to X^*$ is then called 'pure star'. The properties of pure star described in Chapter 3, Problem 5.1 and Theorem 1.20, immediately give the following proposition.

Proposition 3.1

Every *-variety closed under product is closed under pure star.

Straubing has proposed examining the converse.

Problem 3.1

Is every *-variety closed under pure star closed under product?

The first stage consists in examining the variety of star-free languages. Pin has obtained for this variety a result which has something in common with Theorem 1.8.

Theorem 3.2

The variety of star-free languages is the smallest variety closed under pure star.

We note that the concatenation product is not mentioned in this statement, which makes the terminology 'star free' somewhat curious.

A code $c \subset A^+$ is called **very pure** (or **circular**) if, for every $u, v \in A, uv, vu \in C^+$ implies $u, v \in C^+$. Very pure codes are related to the variety $\mathscr{L}t$ of locally testable languages.

Theorem 3.3 (De Luca–Restivo)

Let C be a finite code. Then C is very pure if and only if the language C^+ is locally testable.

Theorem 3.4 (Pin)

The variety $\mathscr{L}t$ is the smallest $+$-variety of languages containing the finite languages and closed under the operation $P \to P^+$ where P is a finite very pure prefix code.

Other restrictions on the operation star have been used by Eilenberg and Schützenberger to describe other varieties of languages. We refer the reader to the books by Eilenberg (*Automata, Languages and Machines*, Vol. B, p. 278) and Lallement (*Semigroups and Combinatorial Applications*, p. 199) for precise statements.

3.2. Varieties described by codes

The statement which follows shows that the syntactic monoids of finite codes allow a good approximation to any finite monoid.

Theorem 3.5 (Margolis–Pin)

For every monoid M there exists a finite prefix code P such that

(a) M divides $M(P^*)$

(b) there exists an aperiodic relational morphism $\tau : M(P^*) \to M$

This theorem justifies the following definition. Let $\mathscr{V}$ be a $*$-variety or $+$-variety of languages and let V be the corresponding variety of monoids or of semigroups respectively. We say that $\mathscr{V}$ is **described** by its finite prefix codes if the variety V can be generated by monoids of the form $M(P^*)$ or by semigroups of the form $S(P^+)$ respectively where P is a finite prefix code. The following can be obtained from Theorems 1.20 and 3.5.

Theorem 3.6

Every $*$-variety closed under product is described by its finite prefix codes.

This is the case in particular for the varieties of rational and star-free languages. The following are other examples.

Theorem 3.7 (Pin)

The $+$-variety of locally testable languages is described by its finite prefix codes.

Theorem 3.8 (Margolis)

The $*$-variety of languages corresponding to Inv is described by its finite prefix codes.

Theorem 3.9 (Margolis–Pin)

Let $H_1, H_2, \ldots, H_n$ be varieties of groups. Then the variety of languages which corresponds to $A * H_1 * A \ldots * A * H_n * A$ is described by its finite prefix codes.

In contrast the varieties of languages corresponding to J, R, DA and B_1 are not described by their finite prefix codes. Schützenberger conjectured that the $+$-variety of languages corresponding to LG was described by its finite codes (see Chapter 2, Problem 3.5).

3.3. Return to the operation $V * W$

Let V and W be varieties of monoids and let $\mathcal{V}$ and $\mathcal{W}$ be the corresponding varieties of languages. A coding $\varphi: A^* \to B^*$ is called a W-coding if $A\varphi$ is a prefix code such that $A^*\varphi \in B^*\mathcal{W}$. In particular an A-coding is called a pure coding for in this case $A\varphi$ is a pure code. The theorem which follows enables us to describe the languages corresponding to $V * W$ when $A^{-1}W = W$, i.e. from Theorem 1.20 when $\mathcal{W}$ is closed under product.

Theorem 3.10 (Margolis–Pin)

Suppose that $W = A^{-1}W$. Then the $*$-variety of languages corresponding to $V * W$ is the smallest variety of languages $\mathcal{U}$ such that for every alphabet A

(1) $A * \mathcal{U}$ contains the languages of the form $L\varphi$ where $\varphi: B^* \to A^*$ is a W-coding and $L \in B^*\mathcal{V}$

(2) if $a \in A$ and $L \in A^*\mathcal{U}$ then $aL \in A^*\mathcal{U}$

Corollary 3.11

The $*$-variety corresponding to $V * A$ is the smallest variety containing $\mathcal{V}$ and closed under pure coding and under left concatenation with letters.

4.   Other results and problems

4.1.   Congruences

Several times we have introduced congruences to define varieties of languages, in particular for the varieties associated with the varieties of monoids or of semigroups J (Chapter 4, Theorem 1.1), R (Chapter 4, Problem 3.2), G_p (Chapter 4, Problem 1.6) and LJ_1 (Theorem 2.1). D. Thérien has developed a general theory which enables us to study this point of view systematically. We can thus describe with the help of congruences the varieties of languages corresponding to A, Com, Gcom, Gsol, Gnil (nilpontent groups), $\bar{G}$sol, $\bar{G}$nil, etc., and introduce new hierarchies.

4.2.   The lattice of varieties

There exists a whose gamut of problems arising from the study of varieties in the sense of Birkhoff. The article of T. Evans (1971) gives a good idea of this type of problem. For example we can study with precision the class of varieties ordered by inclusion: the existence of minimal or maximal elements, of infinite ascending or descending chains, etc. We have thus the following theorem.

Theorem 4.1

The minimal (non-trivial) varieties of monoids are the varieties J_1 and $(\mathbb{Z}_p)$ for p prime. The minimal varieties of semigroups are $(J_1)_S$, K_1, K^r_1, Nil_2 and $(\mathbb{Z}_p)_S$ for p prime.

A variety of monoids V is called **maximal** if $V \neq M$ and if $V \subset W \subset M$ implies $W = V$ or $W = M$. We define likewise maximal varieties of semigroups.

Theorem 4.2 (Margolis)

There does not exist a maximal variety.

Theorem 4.3 (Margolis–Pin)

A variety of monoids which contains a non-commutative monoid contains either a non-commutative group or one of the syntactic monoids $M(A^*a)$, $M(aA^*)$ or $M(ab)$ over the alphabet $A = \{a, b\}$.

In other words there exist only three non-commutative minimal aperiodic varieties. We know also that there exists a non-denumerable infinity of varieties of semigroups contained in Nil and a non-denumerable infinity of varieties of monoids contained in J. We know also a complete description of the varieties contained in the variety of idempotent semigroups, etc.

Another type of problem concerns the equations defining a variety. We saw in Chapter 2 that every variety of semigroups or of monoids generated by a single semigroup was defined by a sequence of equations. In most of the examples which we encountered, this sequence of equations is finite. Nevertheless the results obtained on varieties in the sense of Birkhoff indicate that we must not rely on intuition for this type of problem.

Bibliographic Notes

First of all we give the headings which should be consulted in *Mathematical Reviews* to keep this bibliography up to date:

08   (in particular B 99) for the equations of varieties;
20 M for the theory of semigroups;
68   (in particular 68 D, 68 F) for the theory of automata and of languages.

Basic references

We give next some basic references.

M. A. Arbib, *Algebraic Theory of Machines, Languages and Semigroups*, Academic Press, New York, 1968.
    This is a collection of articles, which are now rather old, on semigroups and automata. Chapters 1 and 7 by J. Rhodes and B. Tilson are a good introduction to finite semigroups. There are several chapters on decompositions in terms of the wreath product.

J. Berstel, *Transductions and Context-free Languages*, Teubner, Stuttgart, 1979.
    This reference might appear to be beyond our subject since it is above all a book concerning context-free languages. However, it is also an excellent reference on rational functions and transductions (Chapters 3 and 4).

J. Berstel, D. Perrin and M. P. Schützenberger, *Theory of Codes*, Academic Press, New York, 1985.
    This is the reference for the theory of variable-length codes. The chapter on unambiguous monoids of relations constitutes a very interesting complement to our Chapter 3.

A. H. Clifford and G. B. Preston, *The Algebraic Theory of Semigroups*, Mathematical Surveys No. 7, American Mathematical Society, Providence, RI, Vol. 1, 1961; Vol. 2, 1967.
    A very detailed book, but already old, on the theory of semigroups.

S. Eilenberg, *Automata, Languages and Machines*, Academic Press, New York, Vol. A, 1974; Vol. B, 1976.
    This is a very rigorous treatise but not always easy of access. Chapters 5–10 of Volume B are entirely devoted to varieties of languages and of semigroups and constitute the basic

reference on this subject. Most of the results of this book, with proofs which are sometimes different (notably for Schützenberger's theorem on star-free languages), can be found there. The other chapters of Volume B are devoted to the wreath product decomposition of semigroups. Chapters 11 and 12, written by B. Tilson, introduce several ideas useful in the theory of semigroups: relational morphisms, the derived semigroup and the Rhodes expansion.

J. M. Howie, *An Introduction to Semigroup Theory*, Academic Press, London, 1976.
An excellent reference for the theory of semigroups.

G. Lallement, *Semigroups and Combinatorial Applications*, Wiley, New York, 1979.
This is also an excellent reference, notably on Green's relations—our Chapter 3 owes much to it. Chapters 6–8 are devoted to recognizable languages and include in particular several interesting characterizations of varieties of languages in Chapter 7.

M. Lothaire, *Combinatorics on Words, Encyclopedia of Mathematics 17*, Addison-Wesley, Reading, MA, 1983.
This is the bible for the combinatorics of free monoids.

Other books

J. Berstel and Ch. Reutenauer, *Les Séries Rationelles et leurs Langages*, Masson, Paris, 1983.
This shows the parallel between rational series and rational languages on the one hand and syntactic algebras and syntactic semigroups on the other.

P. M. Cohn, *Universal Algebra, Mathematics and its Applications 6*, Reidel, Dordrecht, 1981.
This gives results on varieties, but in the sense of Birkhoff. This new edition also includes a chapter on the theory of languages.

J. H. Conway, *Regular Algebra and Finite Machines*, Chapman and Hall, London, 1971.
This is a little-known book which contains unpublished results, notably on rational expressions. Unfortunately the author's very personal terminology makes it very difficult of access.

R. L. Graham, B. L. Rothschild and J. H. Spencer, *Ramsey Theory*, Wiley, New York, 1980.
Everything you want to know about Ramsey's theorem ... except for applications to semigroups.

R. McNaughton and S. Papert, *Counter-free Automata*, MIT Press, Cambridge, MA, 1971.
The link between automata, networks and logic for star-free languages is found here.

H. Neumann, *Varieties of Groups*, Ergebnisse der Mathematik–Springer, Berlin, 1967.
This is a book on group varieties in the sense of Birkhoff but a certain number of results can be adapted for varieties in the sense of Eilenberg.

Articles giving general surveys of an area

These articles can be considered as a complement to Chapter 5.

J. A. Brzozowski, Open problems about regular languages. In R. V. Book (ed.), *Formal Language Theory, Perspectives and Open Problems*, Academic Press, New York, 1980, pp. 23–47.

J. A. Brzozowski, Developments in the theory of regular languages. *Proc. IFIP Congr. 1980*.

T. Evans, The lattice of semigroup varieties, *Semigroup Forum*, **2** (1971) 1–43.

S. W. Margolis, An invitation to finite semigroups—some results and open problems, *Proc. Nebraska Conf. on Semigroups, University of Nebraska, Lincoln, NE, 1980*, pp. 58–81.

J. E. Pin, Concatenation hierarchies, decidability results and problems. In L. J. Cummings (ed.), *Proc. Conf. on Combinatorics on Words, Progress and Perspectives*, Academic Press, New York, 1983, pp. 195–228.

Specialized articles

J. Almeida, Some order properties of the lattice of varieties of commutative semigroups, *Can. J. Math.*, to be published.

J. Almeida, Minimal non-permutative pseudo varieties of semigroups, I and II, *Pac. J. Math.*, to be published.

J. Almeida, Minimal non-permutative pseudo varieties of semigroups, III, *Algebra Universalis*, to be published.

J. Almeida, Power pseudo varieties of semigroups, I and II, to be published.

J. Almeida and N. R. Reilly, Generalized varieties of commutative and nilpotent semigroups, *Semigroup Forum*, **30** (1984) 77–98.

C. J. Ash, Finite semigroups with commuting idempotents, to be published.

G. Birkhoff, On the structures of abstract algebras, *Proc. Cambridge Philos. Soc.*, **31** (1935) 433–454.

A. P. Biryukov, Varieties of idempotent semigroups, *Algebra Logik.*, **9** (1970) 255–273.

J. M. Boé, Représentation des monoïdes. Applications à la théorie des codes, *Thèse de 3ème cycle*, Montpellier, 1976.

R. Brandl, Zur Theorie der Untergruppenabgeschlossenen Formationen: Endliche Varietäten, *J. Algebra*, **73** (1981) 1–22.

J. A. Brzozowski, Hierarchies of aperiodic languages, *RAIRO Inf. Theor.*, **10** (1976) 33–49.

J. A. Brzozowski and F. E. Fich, Languages of R-trivial monoids, *J. Comput. Syst. Sci.*, **20** (1980) 32–49.

J. A. Brzozowski and R. Knast, The dot-depth hierarchy of star-free languages is infinite, *J. Comput. Syst. Sci.*, **16** (1978) 37–55.

J. A. Brzozowski and I. Simon, Characterizations of locally testable events, *Discrete Math.*, **4** (1973) 243–271.

J. R. Büchi, Weak second-order arithmetic and finite automata, *Z. Math. Logik Grundlagen Math.*, **6** (1960) 66–92.

R. S. Cohen and J. A. Brzozowski, On star-free events, *Proc. Hawaii Int. Conf. on System Science, Honolulu, 1968*, pp. 1–4.

R. S. Cohen and J. A. Brzozowski, Dot-depth of star-free events, *J. Comput. Syst. Sci.*, **5** (1971) 1–15.

F. G. Cousineau, J. F. Perrot and J. M. Rifflet, APL programs for direct computation of a finite semigroup. In *APL Congress 73*, North-Holland, Amsterdam, 1973, pp. 67–74.

A. De Luca, On some properties of the syntactic semigroup of very pure subsemigroups, *RAIRO Inf. Théor.*, **14** (1980) 39–56.

A. De Luca, D. Perrin, A. Restivo and S. Termini, Synchronization and simplification, *Discrete Math.*, **27** (1979) 297–308.

A. De Luca and A. Restivo, A characterization of strictly locally testable languages and its application to subsemigroups of a free semigroup, *Inf. Control*, **44** (1980) 300–319.

J. Doyen, Equipotence et unicité de systèmes générateurs minimaux dans certains monoïdes, *Semigroup Forum*, **28** (1984) 341–346.

C. C. Edmunds, On certain finitely based varieties of semigroups, *Semigroup Forum*, **15** (1977) 21–39.

S. Eilenberg and M. P. Schützenberger, On pseudovarieties, *Adv. Math.*, **19** (1976) 413–418.

C. C. Elgot, Decision problems of finite automata design and related arithmetics, *Trans. Am. Math. Soc.*, **98** (1961) 21–52.

F. E. Fich, Languages of *R*-trivial and related monoids, *M. Math. Thesis*, University of Waterloo, 1978.

F. E. Fich and J. A. Brzozowski, A characterization of a dot-depth two analogue of generalized definite languages, *Proc. 6th ICALP, Lecture Notes in Computer Science 71*, Springer, Berlin, 1979, pp. 230–244.

J. A. Gerhard, The lattice of equational classes of idempotent semigroups, *J. Algebra*, **15** (1970) 195–224.

A. Ginzburg, About some properties of definite, reverse definite and related automata, *IEEE Trans. Electron. Comput.*, **15** (1966) 806–810.

R. Graham, On finite 0-simple semigroups and graph theory, *Math. Syst. Theory*, **2** (1968) 325–339.

K. Hashiguchi and N. Honda, Homomorphisms that preserve star height, *Inf. Control*, **30** (1976) 247–266.

K. Hashiguchi and N. Honda, Properties of code events and homomorphisms over regular events, *J. Comput. Syst. Sci.*, **12** (1976) 352–367.

J. Jezek, Intervals in the lattice of varieties, *Algebra Universalis*, **6** (1976) 147–158.

J. Karnofsky and J. Rhodes, Decidability of complexity one-half for finite semigroups, *Semigroup Forum*, **24** (1982) 55–66.

M. Keenan and G. Lallement, On certain codes admitting inverse semigroups as syntactic monoids, *Semigroup Forum*, **8** (1974) 312–331.

K. H. Kim and F. Roush, The semigroup of adjacency patterns of words. In G. Pollack (ed.), *Algebraic Theory of Semigroups*, North-Holland, Amsterdam, 1979, pp. 281–297.

S. C. Kleene, Representation of events in nerve nets and finite automata. In C. E. Shannon and J. McCarthy (eds.), *Automata Studies*, Princeton University Press, Princeton, NJ, 1954, pp. 3–41.

E. I. Kleiman, On basis of identities of Brandt semigroups, *Semigroup Forum*, **13** (1977) 209–218.

E. I. Kleiman, Bases of identities of varieties of inverse semigroups, *Sib. Mat. Zh.*, **20** (4)

(1979) 760–777.

R. Knast, Some theorems on graph congruences, *RAIRO Inf. Théor.*, **17** (1983) 331–342.

R. Knast, A semigroup characterization of dot-depth one languages, *RAIRO Inf. Théor.*, **17** (1983) 321–330.

R. E. Ladner, Application of model-theoretic games to discrete linear orders and finite automata, *Inf. Control*, **33** (1977) 281–303.

G. Lallement, Regular semigroups with $\mathcal{D} = \mathcal{R}$ as syntactic monoids of finite prefix codes, *Theor. Comput. Sci.*, **3** (1977) 35–49.

G. Lallement, Cyclotomic polynomials and unions of groups, *Discrete Math.*, **24** (1978) 19–36.

G. Lallement and E. Milito, Recognizable languages and finite semilattices of groups, *Semigroup Forum*, **11** (1975) 181–185.

E. Le Rest and M. Le Rest, Sur les relations entre un nombre fini de mots, *Thèse 3ème Cycle*, Rouen, 1979.

E. Le Rest and M. Le Rest, Une représentation fidèle des groupes d'un monoïde de relations binaires sur un ensemble fini, *Semigroup Forum*, **21** (1980) 167–172.

E. Le Rest and M. Le Rest, Sur le calcul du monoïde syntaxique d'un sousmonoïde finement engendré, *Semigroup Forum*, **21** (1980) 173–185.

E. Le Rest and S. W. Margolis, On the group complexity of a finite language, *Lecture Notes in Computer Science 154*, Springer, Berlin, 1983, pp. 433–444.

S. W. Margolis, On M-varieties generated by power monoids, *Semigroup Forum*, **22** (1981) 339–353.

S. W. Margolis, On the syntactic transformation semigroup of the language generated by a finite biprefix code, *Theor. Comput. Sci.*, **21** (1982) 225–230.

S. W. Margolis, On the maximal varieties of finite monoids, to be published.

S. W. Margolis and J. E. Pin, Minimal noncommutative varieties and power varieties, *Pac. J. Math.*, **111** (1984) 125–135.

S. W. Margolis and J. E. Pin, Power monoids and finite J-trivial monoids, *Semigroup Forum*, **29** (1984) 99–108.

S. W. Margolis and J. E. Pin, Graphs, inverse semigroups and languages. In *Proc. 1984 Marquette Semigroup Conference, 1984*, pp. 85–112.

S. W. Margolis and J. E. Pin, Varieties of finite monoids and topology for the free monoid. In *Proc. 1984 Marquette Semigroup Conference, 1984*, pp. 113–130.

S. W. Margolis and J. E. Pin, Languages and inverse semigroups. *11th ICALP., Lecture Notes in Computer Science 172*, Springer, Berlin, 1984, pp. 337–346.

S. W. Margolis and J. E. Pin, Product of group languages. *FCT'85, Lecture Notes in Computer Science 199*, Springer, Berlin, 1985, pp. 285–299.

S. W. Margolis and J. E. Pin, Finite inverse semigroups, varieties and languages, to be published.

S. W. Margolis and J. E. Pin, On varieties of rational languages and variable-length codes, II, *J. Pure Appl. Algebra*, to be published.

R. McNaughton, Algebraic decision procedures for local testability, *Math. Syst. Theor.*, **8** (1974) 60–76.

A. R. Meyer, A note on star-free events, *J. Assoc. Comput. Mach.*, **16** (1969) 220–225.

J. Myhill, Finite automata and the representation of events, *Wright Air Development Command Tech. Rep. 57–624*, 1957, pp. 112–137.

E. Nelson, The lattice of equational classes of commutative semigroups, *Can. J. Math.*, **33** (1971) 875–895.

A. Nerode, Linear automaton transformations, *Proc. Am. Math. Soc.*, **9** (1958) 541–544.

P. Perkins, Bases for equational theories of semigroups, *J. Algebra*, **11** (1968) 298–314.

M. Perles, M. O. Rabin and E. Shamir, The theory of definite automata, *IEEE Trans. Electron. Comput.*, **12** (1963) 233–243.

D. Perrin, Sur certains semigroupes syntaxiques, *Séminaires de l'IRIA, Logiques et Automates, Paris, 1971*, pp. 169–177.

D. Perrin, Sur les groupes dans les monoïdes finis. In A. De Luca (ed.), *Proc. Noncommutative Methods in Algebraic and Geometric Combinatorics*, pp. 27–45.

D. Perrin, Variétés de semigroupes et mots infinis, *Lecture Notes in Computer Science 154*, Springer, Berlin, 1983, pp. 610–616.

D. Perrin and J. F. Perrot, A propos des groupes dans certains monoïdes syntaxiques, *Lecture Notes in Mathematics 855*, Springer, Berlin, 1980, pp. 82–91.

D. Perrin and J. E. Pin, First order logic and star-free sets, *J. Comput. Syst. Sci.*, to be published.

D. Perrin and J. E. Pin, On the expressive power of temporal logic, to be published.

J. F. Perrot, Contribution à l'étude des monoïdes syntactiques et de certains groupes associés aux automates finis, *Thèse d'Etat*, Paris, 1972.

J. F. Perrot, Variétés de langages et opérations, *Theor. Comput. Sci.*, **7** (1978) 197–210.

J. E. Pin, Sur le monoïde syntactique de L^* lorsque L est un langage fini, *Theor. Comput. Sci.*, **7** (1978) 211–215.

J. E. Pin, Une caractérisation de trois variétés de langages bien connues, *Lecture Notes in Computer Science 67*, Springer, Berlin, 1979, pp. 233–243.

J. E. Pin, Variétés de langages et monoïde des parties, *Semigroup Forum*, **20** (1980) 11–47.

J. E. Pin, Propriétés syntactiques du produit non ambigu, *Lecture Notes in Computer Science 85*, Springer, Berlin, 1980, pp. 483–499.

J. E. Pin, Variétés de langages et variétés de semigroupes, *Thèse d'Etat*, Paris, 1981.

J. E. Pin, Langages reconnaissables et codage préfixe pur, *Lecture Notes in Computer Science 115*, Springer, Berlin, 1981, pp. 184–192.

J. E. Pin, On varieties of rational languages and variable-length codes, *J. Pure Appl. Algebra*, **23** (1982) 169–196.

J. E. Pin, Arbres et hiérarchies de concaténation, *Lecture Notes in Computer Science 154*, Springer, Berlin, 1983, pp. 617–628.

J. E. Pin, On semidirect products of two finite semilattices, *Semigroup Forum*, **28** (1984) 73–81.

J. E. Pin, Semigroupe des parties et relations de Green, *Can. J. Math.*, **36** (1984) 327–343.

J. E. Pin, Hiérarchies de concaténation, *RAIRO Inf. Théor.*, **18** (1984) 23–46.

J. E. Pin, Finite group topology and p-adic topology for free monoids. *12th ICALP, Lecture Notes in Computer Science 199*, Springer, Berlin, 1985, pp. 285–299.

J. E. Pin, Languages rationnels et reconnaissables, to be published.

J. E. Pin and J. Sakarovitch, Operations and transductions that preserve rationality, *6th GI Conf., Lecture Notes in Computer Science 145*, Springer, Berlin, 1983, pp. 277–288.

J. E. Pin and J. Sakarovitch, Une application de la représentation matricielle des transductions, *Theor. Comput. Sci.*, **35** (1985) 271–293.

J. E. Pin and H. Straubing, Remarques sur le dénombrement des variétés de monoïdes finis, *C.R. Acad. Sci., Sér. A*, **292** (1981) 111–113.

J. E. Pin and H. Straubing, Monoids of upper triangular matrices. In *Colloquia Mathematica Societatis Janos Bolyai, 39, Semigroups, Szeged, 1981*, pp. 259–272.

J. E. Pin, H. Straubing and D. Thérien, Small varieties of finite semigroups and extensions, *J. Aust. Math. Soc.*, **37** (1984) 269–281.

J. E. Pin, H. Straubing and D. Thérien, Locally trivial categories and unambiguous concatenation, to be published.

M. S. Putcha, Subgroups of the power semigroup of a finite semigroup, *Can. J. Math.*, **31** (1979) 1077–1083.

M. O. Rabin and D. Scott, Finite automata and their decision problems, *IBM J. Res. Dev.*, **3** (1959) 114–125.

A. Restivo, Codes and aperiodic languages, *Lecture Notes in Computer Science 2*, Springer, Berlin, 1973, pp. 175–181.

A. Restivo, On a question of McNaughton and Papert, *Inf. Control*, **25** (1974) 93–101.

A. Restivo, A combinatorial property of codes having finite synchronization delay, *Theor. Comput. Sci.*, **1** (1975) 95–101.

Ch. Reutenauer, Sur les variétés de langages et de monoïdes, *Lecture Notes in Computer Science 67*, Springer, Berlin, 1979, pp. 260–265.

Ch. Reutenauer, Une topologie du monoïde libre, *Semigroup Forum*, **18** (1979) 33–49.

Ch. Reutenauer, Séries formelles et algèbres syntactiques, *J. Algebra*, **66** (1980) 448–483.

G. Rindone, Groupes finis et monoïdes syntaxiques, *Thèse 3ème Cycle*, Paris VII, 1983.

M. V. Sapir and E. V. Sukhanov, On manifolds of periodic semigroups, *Izv. Vyssh. Uchebn. Zaved. Mat.*, **25** (4) (1981) 48–55.

M. P. Schützenberger, On an application of semigroup methods to some problems in coding, *IRE Trans. Inf. Theory*, **2** (1956) 47–60.

M. P. Schützenberger, On finite monoids having only trivial subgroups, *Inf. Control*, **8** (1965) 190–194.

M. P. Schützenberger, On a question concerning certain free submonoids, *J. Comb. Theory*, **1** (1966) 437–442.

M. P. Schützenberger, Sur certaines variétés de monoïdes finis. In E. R. Caianiello (ed.), *Automata Theory*, Academic Press, New York, 1966, pp. 314–319.

M. P. Schützenberger, Sur les monoïdes finis dont les groupes sont commutatifs, *RAIRO Inf. Theor.*, **1** (1974) 55–61.

M. P. Schützenberger, Sur certaines pseudo-variétés de monoïdes finis, *IRIA-Laboria Rapport de Recherche 62*, 1974.

M. P. Schützenberger, Sur certaines opérations de fermeture dans les langages rationnels, *Ist. Naz. Alta Math. Symp. Math.*, **15** (1975) 245–253.

M. P. Schützenberger, Sur le produit de concatenation non ambigu, *Semigroup Forum*, **13** (1976) 47–75.

M. P. Schützenberger, A property of finitely generated submonoids of free monoids. In G. Pollack (ed.), *Algebraic Theory of Semigroups*, North-Holland, Amsterdam, 1979, pp. 545–576.

I. Simon, Hierarchies of events dot-depth one, *Ph. D. Thesis*, University of Waterloo, 1972.

I. Simon, Piecewise testable events, *Proc. 2nd GI Conf., Lecture Notes in Computer Science 33*, Springer, Berlin, 1975, pp. 214–222.

I. Simon, Conditions de finitude pour des semigroupes, *C. R. Acad. Sci., Sér. A*, **290** (1980) 1081–1082.

P. Stiffler, Extension of the fundamental theorem of finite semigroups, *Adv. Math.*, **11** (1973) 159–209.

H. Straubing, Varieties of recognizable sets whose syntactic monoids contain solvable groups, *Ph. D. Thesis*, University of California, Berkeley, CA, 1978.

H. Straubing, Families of recognizable sets corresponding to certain varieties of finite monoids, *J. Pure Appl. Algebra*, **15** (1979) 305–318.

H. Straubing, Aperiodic homomorphisms and the concatenation product of recognizable sets, *J. Pure Appl. Algebra*, **15** (1979) 319–327.

H. Straubing, Recognizable sets and power sets of finite semigroups, *Semigroup Forum*, **18** (1979) 331–340.

H. Straubing, On finite *J*-trivial monoids, *Semigroup Forum*, **19** (1980) 107–110.

H. Straubing, A generalization of the Schützenberger product of finite monoids, *Theor. Comput. Sci.*, **13** (1981) 137–150.

H. Straubing, Relational morphisms and operations on recognizable sets, *RAIRO Inf. Théor.*, **15** (1981) 149–159.

H. Straubing, The variety generated by finite nilpotent monoids, *Semigroup Forum*, **24** (1982) 25–38.

H. Straubing, Finite semigroup varieties of the form $V*D$, *J. Pure Appl. Algebra*, **36** (1985) 53–94.

H. Straubing, Semigroups and languages of dot-depth two, to be published.

H. Straubing and D. Thérien, Partially ordered finite monoids and a theorem of I. Simon, to be published.

D. Thérien, Languages of nilpotent and solvable groups, *Lecture Notes in Computer Science 71*, Springer, Berlin, 1979, pp. 616–632.

D. Thérien, Classification of regular languages by congruences, *Ph.D. Thesis*, University of Waterloo, 1980.

D. Thérien, Classification of finite monoids: the language approach, *Theor. Comput. Sci.*, **14** (1981) 195–208.

D. Thérien, Recognizable languages and congruences, *Semigroup Forum*, **23** (1981) 371–373.

D. Thérien, Sur les monoïdes dont tous les groupes sont résolubles, *Semigroup Forum*, **26** (1983) 89–101.

D. Thérien, Subword counting and nilpotent groups. In L. J. Cummings (ed.), *Proc. Conf. on Combinatorics on Words, Progress and Perspectives*, Academic Press, New York, 1983, pp. 297–306.

D. Thérien, A language theoretic interpretation of Schützenberger representations, *Semigroup Forum*, **28** (1984) 235–248.

D. Thérien and A. Weiss, Graph congruences and wreath products, *J. Pure Appl. Algebra*, **36** (1985) 205–215.

W. Thomas, Star-free regular sets of ω-sequences, *Inf. Control*, **42** (1979) 148–156.

W. Thomas, Classifying regular events in symbolic logic, *J. Comput. Syst. Sci.*, **25** (1982) 360–376.

B. Tilson, Complexity of two $\mathscr{J}$-class semigroups, *Adv. Math.*, **11** (1973) 215–237.

B. Tilson, in S. Eilenberg, *Automata, Languages and Machines*, Academic Press, New York, Vol. B, 1976, Chapters 11 and 12.

B. Tilson, Categories as algebras: an essential ingredient in the theory of semigroups, to be published.

A. V. Tishchenko, The finiteness of a base of identities for five-element monoids, *Semigroup Forum*, **20** (1980) 171–186.

A. N. Trakhtman, The basis of identities of the five element Brandt semigroup, *Issled. Sovrem. Algebre, Mat. Zap.*, **12** (3) (1982) 147–149.

A. Weiss, The local and global varieties induced by nilpotent monoids, *RAIRO Inf. Theor. Appl.*, to be published.

A. Weiss and D. Thérien, Varieties of finite categories, *RAIRO Inf. Theor. Appl.*, to be published.

C. Wells, Some applications of the wreath product construction, *Am. Math. Mon.*, **83** (1976) 317–338.

Y. Zalcstein, Locally testable languages, *J. Comput. Syst. Sci.*, **6** (1972) 151–167.

Y. Zalcstein, Locally testable semigroups, *Semigroup Forum*, **5** (1973) 151–167.

Y. Zalcstein, Syntactic semigroups of some classes of star-free languages. In M. Nivat (ed.), *Automata, Languages and Programming*, North-Holland, Amsterdam, 1973, pp. 135–144.

Index